The Marathon Monks
of Mount Hiei

RIDER

Ajari Sakai Yūsai, veteran of two 1,000-day marathons, on the
Imuro Valley Course. (Photo courtesy of Fudō-dō)

The Marathon Monks
of Mount Hiei

John Stevens

PHOTOGRAPHS BY
TADASHI NAMBA

RIDER
RIDER
LONDON SYDNEY AUCKLAND JOHANNESBURG

First published in the UK in 1989 by Rider
An imprint of Century Hutchinson Ltd
Brookmount House, 62-65 Chandos Place, Covent Garden, London WC2N 4NW

Century Hutchinson Australia (Pty) Ltd
89-91 Albion Street, Surry Hills, NSW 2010, Australia

Century Hutchinson New Zealand Ltd
PO Box 40-086, 32-34 View Road, Glenfield, Auckland 10, New Zealand

Century Hutchinson South Africa (Pty) Ltd
PO Box 337, Bergvlei 2012, South Africa
First published in the USA by Shambhala Publications Inc 1988

Printed and bound in the United States of America
by Edwards Brothers Inc, Ann Arbor, Michigan

British Library Cataloguing in Publication data

Stevens, John, *1947–*
    The marathon monks of Mount Hiei.
    1. Japan. Zen Buddhism. Monks.
    I. Title
    294.3′657′0952

ISBN-0-7126-1865-1

Contents

Preface

*I*T MAY WELL BE that the greatest athletes today are not the stars of professional sports, nor the Olympic champions, nor the top triathlon competitors, but the marathon monks of Japan's Mount Hiei. The amazing feats and the incredible endurance of these "Running Buddhas" are likely unrivaled in the annals of athletic endeavor. And the prize they seek to capture consists not of such trifles as a pot of gold or a few fleeting moments of glory, but enlightenment in the here and now—the greatest thing a human being can achieve.

This book is about these superlative spiritual athletes; Hiei, the magic mountain on which they train; and Tendai Buddhism, the philosophy that inspires and sustains them in their quest for the supreme. The wonderful photographs used to illustrate this work were taken by Tadashi Namba, who is something of a marathon monk himself. As a teenager on a visit to Kyoto, Namba was so impressed with the bearing of the marathon monk Utsumi Shunshō,* whom he happened to encounter on one of that priest's jaunts through the city, that he made his way to Hiei and became a lay monk at Myō-ō-dō, the main training temple. His primary religious practice for the past decade has been to record the exploits of the marathon monks on film, joining them on their nightly runs and observing them as they defied death in their long prayer fasts and as they interacted with the world as emissaries of the highest form of Tendai Buddhism. Thus, Namba is particularly sensitive to all aspects of the life of a marathon monk, and his photographs reveal the practice from within, possessing a subtlety that a mere technician, no matter how proficient, could never equal.

* With the exception of the name of the photographer, Tadashi Namba, Japanese names in this book are given in the traditional manner, family name first.

Part One, "The World of Tendai Buddhism," is directed toward students seeking specific information on Tendai Buddhism and traditional Japanese religious culture. Part Two, "The Marathon Monks," is geared for those readers with a more general interest in the world of the spirit, psychophysical training, and the splendors of human endeavor. References for academic specialists are contained in the footnotes and bibliography. In short, this book is a typical example of Tendai universalism, with something for everyone! Readers will probably benefit the most by reading the exciting Part Two first for stimulation and inspiration and then perusing the denser Part One for historical background and a deeper perspective on Tendai Buddhism, an important subject not well known in the West.

It is my sincere hope that the reader will come to share the conviction of the marathon monks: "If mind and body are unified, there is nothing that cannot be accomplished. Strive to attain the ultimate, and the universe will someday be yours!"

THE WORLD OF TENDAI BUDDHISM

To a practitioner of Tendai, everything is wonderful.
—*Traditional proverb*

THE TREASURE OF A NATION

Saichō, Founder of Japanese Tendai

What is the treasure of a nation? A person with a mind set on the Way. One with such a mind is a true treasure. The ancients have said that a nation's wealth does not consist of a heap of precious stones. One virtuous individual who illuminates a thousand leagues is a national treasure. The old philosophers stated clearly, "One who speaks but does not act is the teacher of a nation. One who acts but does not speak is the foundation of a nation. One who both speaks and acts is the treasure of a nation."[1]—*Saichō*

T HE DEVOUT BUDDHIST Mitsuno-obito-Kiyoshi and his wife, Fujiwara Tōshi (Fujiko), longed for a child for years without success. Kiyoshi, whose ancestors had immigrated from China generations ago, decided to seclude himself on the sacred peak of Hiei and fast and pray in the hope of receiving the blessing of a child. After climbing through the thick mountain forest, Kiyoshi was drawn to a fragrant clearing. There he erected a makeshift hut and embarked on a seven-day fast. On the fourth day of the fast, Kiyoshi had a vision—surely, he thought, an

◄ Saichō, the Patriarch of Tendai Buddhism, in deep meditation, "calming the mind and discerning the real." He is depicted wearing a hood that, according to legend, was sent by the emperor to help protect the master against the dreadful cold of the "frozen peak," Mount Hiei.

auspicious omen. And it was, for later in that year of 766, on the eighteenth day of the eighth month, his wife gave birth to a splendid son.[2]

The aristocratic parents lavished care and attention on their only child, providing him with the finest books and tutors. The clever boy made rapid progress in his studies and also displayed considerable skill at wood-carving. Kiyoshi had previously converted part of his home into a temple, and the boy quickly came to share his father's ardent interest in Buddhism. In 780, around age fourteen, the lad received preliminary ordination (*tokudō*) from the priest Gyōhō at the Ōmi Kokubun-ji monastery, not far from his home. The new monk received the name Saichō, meaning "Highest Clarity."[3]

Gyohō was an eminent teacher and practitioner in an age when corruption in religion was widespread. Buddhism had been introduced officially into Japan in 552 (or 538 according to another account) when the king of the Korean kingdom of Paikche presented the Japanese emperor with sutras, an image of Śākyamūni Buddha, and other Buddhist paraphernalia. This kind of transmission was typical, for in its initial phase Buddhism tends to be a religion largely for the upper classes. For an order of mendicants to exist, there must be wealthy patrons to provide food, clothing, and shelter and a sympathetic government to sanction the monks' exemption from taxation and military service. As one early text states, "It is difficult for Buddhism to maintain itself without the support of a king."[4] Thus the spread of Buddhism from India to China to Korea and thence to Japan was accomplished primarily by traders, aristocrats, and well-subsidized monks who gravitated toward urban centers, the places in which power, money, and influence were concentrated.

Naturally, such well-off benefactors were most attracted to the material benefits to be accrued from professing Buddhism. Thus, the Korean king informed the Japanese emperor that Buddhism was a miraculous creed that could grant his every wish. Members of the Japanese court for the most part had little interest in the subtleties of Buddhist practice and thought; their main concern was the efficacy of Buddhism in preventing calamity and fostering prosperity. While aristocrats and wealthy landowners were somewhat shielded from the dangers posed by thieves, marauding soldiers, and famine, they were powerless in the face of floods, fires, earthquakes, and, above all, sickness and death. The majority of early Japanese Buddhists worshiped the Buddhist images as idols and regarded Buddhist monks and nuns as shamans. Many of the first temples were established in order to effect the cure of some ailing member of the imperial family, and if the cure did not occur,

Buddha images might well be torn unceremoniously from their pedestals and cast into the sea.

Early Buddhism in Japan was thus employed, first of all, as an instrument to protect aristocrats in particular and the nation in general. Its second function was to promote learning and culture. From the sixth to the eighth century, Buddhist culture was imported to Japan in full force, culminating in the grand "Temple Buddhism" of Nara, the new capital of Japan patterned after T'ang China's cosmopolitan city of Chang'an. During this period, dozens of outstanding Korean, Chinese, Central Asian, and Indian teachers journeyed to Japan to offer instruction in the material and spiritual arts of Buddhism, and selected Japanese were sent to the mainland to study. A millennium of Asian Buddhist culture was thus imported into Japan in a little more than two hundred years, although it took several more centuries to assimilate it completely.

Temple Buddhism was State Buddhism: The Dharma was a possession of the government, to be utilized to safeguard the nation and also "advertise" Japan's increasing sophistication. In that period in the Far East, nations were judged by the level of their Buddhist culture, and each country competed to build the biggest, the best, and the most beautiful—hence Emperor Shōmu's fervent support, in 749, of the construction of Tōdai-ji (still the world's largest wooden building at two-thirds its original size) and the casting of the temple's Great Buddha—an image so colossal that it required 100 million tons of copper. Later, Emperor Shōmu established the Kokunbun-ji system, decreeing that each province should maintain at public expense a National Temple staffed with monks and nuns to copy and recite Buddhist sutras for the protection of the nation and the elimination of evil.

Unfortunately, the heady worldly success of Buddhism in Japan—at the height of its prosperity Tōdai-ji employed 4,000 peasants and 100 slaves to farm its massive land holdings—had a corrupting effect on some of the religion's adherents. A primary example of this was the infamous Dōkyō, the monk who would be emperor. Dōkyō, affiliated with Tōdai-ji, was a handsome, charismatic man with a profound knowledge of esoteric rites and astrology. He ingratiated himself with the retired Empress Kōken, daughter of Shōmu and a pious Buddhist herself, by curing her (likely psychosomatic) illness. Thereafter, Dōkyō had free access to her inner chambers, and, after Kōken reassumed the throne at Dōkyō's urging, he persuaded the spellbound empress to promote him to higher and higher positions within the government hierarchy. He then attempted to have Kōken name him as her successor, but she hesitated in the face of fierce opposition. When Dōkyō's patroness died in 770, he was finally ousted from power and exiled to die in disgrace.

Of course, not every Buddhist in Japan at the time was a charlatan, religious bureaucrat, or cloistered scholar; there was always a small core of dedicated and thoughtful practitioners who took the Dharma seriously and strove to manifest Buddhism in daily life. Among these was the Prince Regent Shōtoku Taishi (574– 622), often called the Father of Japanese Buddhism, who initially misconstrued Buddhism as an incantatory religion but later grasped its deeper meaning through diligent study and reflection. His poignant last words were, reportedly, "This world is empty and vain; Buddha alone is true." Then there was the "Bodhisattva" monk Gyōgi (668–748). Unlike the other priests, who occupied themselves fruitlessly with arcane studies and performing elaborate rites for the benefit of noblemen, Gyōgi was intent on the salvation of all the people in Japan. He was famed for his selfless devotion to the common folk and his public works: erecting bridges, constructing roads, digging wells, ponds, and canals, building boat landings, clearing land for cultivation, setting up homes for the dispossessed, and tending the sick and needy. Significantly, the government did not care for such activists as Gyōgi—who, among other things, protested against excessive taxation—and he was under a constant threat of exile or other punishment.

Saichō's master Gyōhō, was another of these "core teachers" who transmitted the essence of Buddhism, free of worldly taint. Gyōhō (722–797) was taught by Dōsen (Tao-hsuan), a Chinese master who arrived in Japan in 736. In addition to being a precept monk (one who strictly followed the monastic rules), Dōsen was also a keen student of Hossō idealism, an experienced Zen practitioner, and an expert chanter of texts, possessing, it is said, a voice "as clear and resonant as a Bodhi- sattva's." Dōsen passed on to Gyōhō this tradition of eclectic scholarship combined with practical implication—the two trained together as hermits for some years— and Gyōhō in turn inspired Saichō.

Since the government strictly controlled all ordinations, every candidate was required to pass a demanding examination that covered classical Buddhist texts, Chinese composition, and rites and procedures, quite similar in fact to the civil service exam for bureaucrats. The studious Saichō had no trouble passing, and, as mentioned above, he took preliminary ordination in 780.

During the next five years Saichō familiarized himself with the teachings of the Six Schools of Nara Buddhism, each representing a different aspect of the Dharma:

there was the *Kusha (Abhidharma-kośa)* school, which analyzed existence in terms of its constituent elements; the *Jōjitsu (Satyasiddhi-śāstra)* school of philosophical investigation into the Truth; the *Ritsu (Vinaya)* school, representing the importance of precepts in Buddhism; the *Sanron (Mādhyamika)* school of transcendental wisdom and cosmic emptiness; the idealist *Hossō (Yogācāra)* school of "mind only"; and the grand *Kegon (Avataṃsaka)* school, which aimed at perceiving the universe in all its manifold harmony.[5]

In 785, at the age of nineteen, Saichō joined a large group of novices and received full ordination at Tōdai-ji. However, instead of following the crowd and pursuing a promising and perhaps lucrative career in the magnificent temples of Nara, the determined young monk suddenly fled the capital for the solitude of Hiei. As a youth, Saichō had spent many days on that sacred peak, contemplating nature and seeking out the hermits and wizards who hid there in caves and huts, practicing religion far removed from the turmoil of the world below. These half-priest, half-layman practitioners subsisted on herbs, mushrooms, nuts, and wild vegetables, covered themselves with robes of bark and rush leaves, and acquired a natural wisdom by communing with the sun, sky, and earth. It is not surprising that a sensitive, idealistic monk would choose to spend his time there among the clouds and trees rather than in the hustle and bustle of a big city. Such an act was, strictly speaking, illegal because monks were not supposed to live in the mountains beyond government control—all the ascetics on Hiei were "irregular mountain priests"—but the rule was not being enforced, by way of encouraging priests to once again concentrate on pure practice instead of politics. Saichō's dramatic move corresponds to a second stage in the development of Buddhism: a shift from urban temple Buddhism to pristine mountain Buddhism, where the Dharma can be studied and practiced in a peaceful, elevating environment.

With the assistance of his family, Saichō threw himself into Buddhist training, "living in caves and grass huts, under the pines and on the top of the cliffs making little of oneself while valuing the Dharma."[6] Clad in a thin robe, subsisting on wild vegetables, herbs, and spring water, the young monk vowed to penetrate the Dharma. A year or two after his seclusion on Hiei, Saichō composed his celebrated "Letter of Resolve" (*Ganmon*):[7]

> This evanescent world is full of suffering and anxiety; every being is constantly troubled and never at ease. The light of Śākyamuni [the

Buddha of the past] has long been hidden, and that of Maitreya [the Buddha of the future] has yet to shine. The dangers of war, pestilence, and famine draw near, and all are engulfed by evil, selfishness, passions, ill fortune, and death. Life is like a stray breeze, difficult to hold, and our bodily existence is like a drop of dew, easy to vanish. There is no place to find shelter, and young and old alike ultimately turn into sun-bleached bones. The grave claims both the noble and the base, and all return to their original elements. No one can escape that fate.

Since we can never partake of the elixir of eternal life, all of us are unsure of our final destiny. The miraculous powers of prolonged existence are eventually futile, and death can come at any time. If we do not create good during our lifetime, at death we will be kindling-wood for hell. The gift of human life is difficult to obtain but so easy to lose. Good intentions are hard to develop and easy to forget. Śākyamuni Buddha compared the difficulty of obtaining human birth to locating a needle sunk in the greatest ocean and threading it with a piece of string lost on the highest mountain. An ancient Chinese king knew well the preciousness of life and never wasted a single minute of his life on frivolous pursuits.

There is no principle that allows one to acquire good *karma* without earning it, nor is there a loophole that permits one to avoid the pangs of hell without doing good in this life. I have reflected on all of this, and I am ashamed at receiving charity without deserving it and deceiving all beings with my ignorance. As it states in the sutras, "Those who give charity ascend to heaven, and those who receive it fall into hell." Lady Dai-i ceaselessly performed good deeds for five bad monks; she was rewarded by being born as Queen Mari, while they were reincarnated as five of her barren female slaves. It is clear from this tale how the law of retribution functions. One who is aware of the origin of suffering but fails to create good is an enemy of Buddha, an armless creature unable to pick up the many treasures the holy teaching offers.

The lowly and insignificant Saichō, among the most foolish, ignorant, and deluded of men, vows never to turn his back on the Buddhas, the nation, or his parents. Despite my limitations, I have made the resolutions listed below. Free of attachment to worldly things, willing to use all means, and intent on achieving the supreme principles, I will be unbending in my resolve.

1. Until I obtain sufficient awakening, I will not leave the mountain or work in the world.
2. Until I illuminate the ultimate principle, I will not indulge in worldly pleasures.
3. Until I grasp the essence of the pure precepts, I will not attend state ceremonies or religious feasts.
4. Until I attain the heart of transcendental wisdom, I will avoid all entanglements.
5. Whatever virtue and wisdom I may accrue through my training will not be for my own sake but for the benefit and supreme liberation of all beings throughout the universe.

Thus I vow not to savor the taste of liberation alone nor realize the fruit of *nirvāṇa* all by myself. All beings in the Dharma world must rise to wonderful awakening and experience the subtle flavor of the Dharma together.

Through the strength of my vows I hope to achieve sufficient awakening, and if I develop spiritual powers I will not use them for selfish purposes, nor will I become attached to enlightenment. I vow always to pursue the unbounded and unlimited four great works {saving all sentient beings, cutting off all evil passions, learning all the principles of the Dharma, and mastering the Buddhist Way][8] throughout my entire life. I will enter the Dharma world, transverse the six realms, forever training and performing Buddha work.

In his intense drive to attain awakening Saichō initially perused such texts as *The Awakening of Faith in the Mahāyāna (Daijō kishin ron)* and the *Garland Sūtra (Avataṃsaka Sūtra)* and their commentaries.[9] Several of those commentaries mentioned the superlative teaching of the T'ien-t'ai (Jap. Tendai) teaching, and Saichō sent a message to his contacts in Nara asking them to search for T'ien-t'ai manuscripts. Although both the precept master Ganjin (Chien-chen, 687–763) and Dōsen had brought T'ien-t'ai texts with them from China, the books failed to arouse much interest in Nara circles, and the manuscripts lay unopened in monastic libraries. Saichō borrowed and copied the texts, becoming immersed in the thought of the Chinese master Chih-i (531–597; known in Japanese as Tendai Daishi).

According to legend, Chih-i was originally a follower of the Ch'an (Zen) school but grew uncomfortable with that sect's uncompromising iconoclasm and rejection of all aids, external and internal. Chih-i favored a more intellectual approach, combining sutra learning and philosophical inquiry with practical meditation. He eventually became famous far and wide for his scholarship and virtue, and was appointed tutor of the crown prince in Nanking. Students flocked to learn from the master, but Chih-i made the following observation: "In my first year of teaching here I had forty students, of which twenty were satisfactory. The next year I had one hundred, but still only twenty were satisfactory and attained the Dharma. The third year I had two hundred students, but this time only ten accomplished anything. It is better to have a few earnest disciples than ten thousand mediocre ones." So saying, Chih-i fled the capital, ignoring the emperor's pleas to remain, and went with a small band of followers to dwell in the solitude of Mount T'ien-t'ai (Jap. Tendai-san).[10]

Home of Taoist immortals, mountain ascetics, and Buddhist hermits, Mount T'ien-t'ai was a magnificent peak of thick forests, deep ravines, and thundering waterfalls, cut off from the world by heavy mist in summer and deep snow in winter. It was thus the ideal locale for the contemplation of the Dharma's profundities.[11] At Kuo-ch'ing, the monastery he founded on T'ien-t'ai, Chih-i expounded his systematic interpretation of Buddhism and its methods for realization.

By Chih-i's time, Buddhism had been established in China for five centuries, with all the major sutras having been translated into the native language. Now that the main doctrines were available in manuscript, however, there was tremendous confusion over the seeming contradictions in the texts themselves and the vast differences in the interpretation and practice of the Dharma. In response to this problem, Chih-i and his disciples formulated the theory of the Five Periods and Eight Doctrines.

The First Period of the Buddha's teaching immediately followed his supreme enlightenment with its cosmic insights into the nature of existence. This is known as the Garland Period, referring to the grand vision of time, space, and being revealed in the *Garland Sūtra*. The Buddha elucidated the full extent of his enlightenment but then realized that no one could understand it, all being as if deaf and dumb. This period lasted three weeks, that is, the ecstatic interval between the Buddha's enlightenment beneath the Bodhi Tree and his return to the world to proclaim the Dharma. This First Period was compared by Chih-i to the brilliant light of dawn illuminating the highest peaks, and to fresh whole milk with all the nutrients intact.

In the Second Period, the Buddha used the accommodated teaching—easy-to-understand doctrines such as the Four Noble Truths and so on—to attract people to the Dharma. In this twelve-year period of "basic Buddhism," all the Hīnayāna doctrines were taught. It is similar to the sun's rays brightening the darkest valleys and to the taking of milk in the more palatable form of cream.

The Third Period, known as the time of development or transition, marked the beginning of the more subtle, broader, and equal teachings. Preliminary Mahāyāna doctrine was advanced, and the Buddha rebuked those followers who stubbornly clung to the Hīnayāna methods. This period lasted eight years and was compared to the gradually ascending morning sun and the tasty butter curds produced by refinement of the cream.

Transcendental Wisdom was the theme of the twenty-two-year Fourth Period. All ideas, concepts, and mental constructions were rejected as being intrinsically empty, and all attachments, even to Buddhism, were to be summarily cast off. This period was a time of selection, exploration, and unification carried out by the Bodhisattvas. Here the sun is at mid-morning and the practitioners partake of the pure cream.

The Fifth Period is that of the *Lotus Sūtra* and its ancillary text, the *Nirvāṇa Sūtra*.[12] In contrast to the negative formulations of the Fourth Period, this one is positive: all the previous teachings are perfected and harmonized by the one vehicle (*ekayāna*). This last stage, symbolized by the final eight years of the Buddha's life (and condensed in the one-day proclamation of the *Nirvāṇa Sūtra*), is a time of opening and coming together. Chih-i selected the *Lotus Sūtra* as the highest manifestation of Buddhism because it declared the universal means of salvation of all beings and the eternal proclamation of the Dharma.

The *Lotus Sūtra* has the entire cosmos as its cast, and the *dramatis personae* run the gamut from the Supreme Buddha to the most depraved denizens of hell. Colossal in scope, the sutra urges all beings to uncover their original, unsullied, indestructible nature and to realize Buddhahood through countless means, as varied and multidimensional as life itself. Here it is now high noon, and those in this stage are nourished by the richest and most delectable *ghee,* or clarified butter, the essence of milk.

Chih-i formulated the notion of Eight Doctrines to further elucidate the nature of the Five Periods:

1. Abrupt: The direct and unadulterated teaching for those few who can immediately and intuitively grasp the Dharma.

2. Gradual: Step-by-step instruction and progressive understanding.

3. Secret: The perception on the part of the listener that he or she alone is receiving the teaching; that is, esoteric, individual understanding.

4. Undetermined: Esoteric teaching offered to all listeners, each one receiving it at a different level of comprehension.

5. *Tripiṭaka* ("Collected Writings"): The sum total of the written teachings for those who study and analyze the texts.

6. Transitional: Aimed at the Hinayanists and lower-level Bodhisattvas, urging them to consider the whole rather than the parts.

7. Special: Pure transcendental wisdom for the advanced Bodhisattvas.

8. Complete: The realized teachings of the Middle Way.

The Five Periods and the Eight Teachings are, of course, metaphoric. The Buddha's message was not unfolded in such a strict chronological fashion; all the periods and teachings are organically related, each reflecting a different facet of Buddhism. Śakyāmuni planted the seeds of the Dharma, which resulted in a continual elaboration of the teachings over the centuries. The above clarification is a type of "skillful means" to make Buddhism easier to comprehend.

The pillar of Chih-i's thought is his presentation of the Three Truths. All elements are characterized by three aspects: (1) the Empty, (2) the Relative, and (3) the Integral.

Emptiness means being free of subjective views, without passionate attachments, and unconditionally unobstructed. In this Truth, existence is perceived as being transcendent, universal, and devoid of attributes. From the standpoint of training, emptiness is the means to break through illusions and to achieve the no-mind of Zen.

Emptiness is not nothingness, however, and one must function on a temporal, relative plane of existence. The Relative allows one to form the "particulars" of existence by giving body to the Empty. This also allows for the establishment of provisional teachings, the elaborate schemes of Tantra, to transmit Buddhist wisdom.

The Integral, literally "The Middle," is a synthesis of the negative and the positive, the universal and the particular, realization and practice. The integral Middle Way—the goal of Tendai—is represented by Śākyamuni, who was totally enlightened yet fully human. Ultimately, on the highest levels, there is mutual penetration: the Three Truths are One, the One Truth is Three. This is stated philosophically: "The Middle Way is identical to the True State of Existence, which is none other than Thusness." Or, more succinctly: "One thought, three thousand worlds." One thought includes all ideas from the highest to the most mundane and embraces all elements of existence from the most minute particle to the grandest universe. It is realization that "One is all, all is one," a summing up of the microcosm and macrocosm in an instant.[13]

Although Chih-i and his later disciples further probed Buddhism in greater detail, classical T'ien-t'ai thought revolves around this central tenet. Intellectual acumen may avail the student a small measure of understanding regarding the above points, but the full ramifications of the Three Truths can only be realized through direct perception. For this Chih-i advocated the practice of *chih-kuan* (Jap. *shikan*). *Chih* (Skt. *śamatha*) is the "stopping" of all mental processes, an intent focusing of one's being in the here and now, an imperturbable state of mind beyond delusive thought. *Kuan* (Skt. *vipaśyanā*) is the "insight" that unfolds as a result of perceiving things as they really are—uncovered, integrated, and whole. Chih-i wrote in his *Meditation Manual (T'ung meng chih-kuan):*[14] "The meditation of Hinayanists is excessive, and that prevents them from seeing Buddha-nature; the wisdom of the highest Bodhisattvas is too powerful, and that hinders their perception of Buddha-nature. All the Buddhas and Tathāgatas have meditation and wisdom in equal measure, and that enables them to clearly see the Buddha-nature." That sentiment echoes a line (verse 372) in the *Dhammapada,* a basic Buddhist text. "Without wisdom there is no meditation and without meditation there is no wisdom; one who has both wisdom and meditation is near *nirvāna.*"

Saichō took Chih-i's system to heart and assiduously practiced *shikan* meditation as well as poring over T'ien-t'ai and a host of other texts. Saichō was able to bring only a few scrolls with him when he first went to Hiei and eventually realized that in order to create a real monastery he would need a collection of the entire Buddhist canon. After securing sufficient funds from his patrons for paper, ink, and brushes, Saichō and his disciples went to work copying the 5,200 volumes of the Buddhist canon plus some 4,000 commentaries. Several of the Nara temples contributed copies made from volumes in their libraries, and within ten years Saichō had enough books on hand to justify the formal establishment of a library on Hiei. In addition to copying hundreds of volumes personally, Saichō also carefully proofread—"One mistake is too many," he believed—all the works copied by his disciples and thus, like all the other great Japanese Patriarchs, absorbed the entire range of Buddhist literature.

Saichō left a very interesting document on the practice of *shakyō* entitled "Admonitions for Sutra Copyists." [15] The short text succinctly conveys the flavor of Saichō's understanding of Buddhism and his ability to combine high ideals with practical application.

ADMONITIONS FOR COPYISTS

The motivation of those Bodhisattvas who have aroused the supreme Buddha-mind and copy the sutras is, first of all, to correctly comprehend the Complete Teaching. In the correct comprehension of the Complete Teaching the three natures—good, bad, neutral—are unified into One Mind. Outside One Mind nothing exists because all elements are contained within it and encompassed by it. With this [One Mind] extinguish all contrary views and seek nonthought. Further, do not fall into the realm of covetousness, anger, or ignorance nor let selfish views arise; always utilize the supreme wisdom of nondiscrimination while functioning in the world of *saṃsāra*. Moving, standing, sitting, lying, speaking, acting—always practice the Middle Way of concentration and insight. This is the correct comprehension of the Complete Teaching of the Middle Way. Is not the complete and abrupt True Way manifest both on sun-drenched peaks and among tenacious weeds?

Three elements are necessary for the practice of the True Path of the Complete Teaching: (1) discipline, (2) meditation, and (3) wisdom. There are hundreds of disciplines and precepts, but the Ten Good Deeds [not to kill, steal, have illicit sex, lie, use improper language, slander, equivocate, covet, get angry, or hold false views] are the best. There are dozens of meditation techniques, but all are based on the One Mind. There are scores of wisdom teachings, but all are derived from the ultimate, unattached wisdom.

It may be asked, "Why do sutra copyists need to follow discipline?"

The answer: When one copies the Mahāyāna sutras and their commentaries, the copyist enters a purified room, sits on an immaculate seat, holds the sutra rolls in the hands, and looks at the characters with the eyes; hence, the copyist must not be the captive of murder, thievery, or lust in deed, word, or thought at any time. Since there is no limit to the virtue accrued through this practice, do not be content with [good behavior] for just a few days, months, or years. [Such] practice involves purification of the body, reflection on past errors, veneration of the Three Treasures, and expounding the Dharma for the benefit of all sentient beings. This is the source of all [Buddhist activities].

To cease evil is to stop it from occurring; to do good is to contemplate [its form]. Further, a copyist of the Mahāyāna sutras must not engage in frivolous talk when working on a sutra. Be careful to keep the mouth closed when copying in order not to stain the text with spittle, lose your place, or skip characters or columns. Cease all inappropriate speech and use only respectful language. To purify the mouth, eliminate words that are abusive, abrasive, alienating, flattering, and the like. Purification of speech also involves the acts of repentance, veneration, proclaiming of the Dharma, and manifold practices mentioned above.

Copyists of the Mahāyāna sutras must rely on the correct comprehension of the Complete Teachings and never habor thoughts of receiving large donations or hope for improved *karma* or enhanced reputations; then they will be separated from covetousness. Relying, too, on the correct comprehension of the Complete Teaching, copyists should not discriminate between self and others nor let resentful thoughts arise; then they will be separated from anger. Nor should they discriminate between different elements of existence. Rely on the nondiscrimination of the Middle Way, leap from the peak of brilliant unborn wisdom, cross the vast sky of One Mind, and illuminate the blackest depths of delusion, bias, and evil by constantly practicing in the manner of Buddha. This is separation from ignorance. With such a realization, consciousness, too, can be quickly purified through the attainment of

One Mind. In this manner, the Ten Evil Deeds of act, word, and thought are eliminated and good actions proliferate. As soon as a good intention occurs internally, the fruit appears externally. This is true purification of deeds, words, and thoughts; it is the greatest of all disciplines, the essence of all pure precepts. Do not create *karma* and you will naturally avoid the need for rigid controls. From this kind of discipline One Mind develops. It enables one to be unaffected by the Three Poisons [greed, lust, anger]. The practice of nondual wisdom is found in such insight.

It may be asked, "Why do copyists need to meditate?"

The answer: When one copies the Mahāyāna sutras it is not permissible to let one's thoughts drift. The One Mind must be settled on each unfolding of the Dharma. One line includes all other lines. Such is the practice of copying with the One Mind of the Perfect Teaching. Accordingly, such meditation will purify the six sense organs, as it states in chapter six of the *Lotus Sūtra:* "Even though the untainted Dharma body is not yet attained, it is still possible to purify the six sense organs." Such is the power of meditation, manifest as all-powerful Diamond *samādhi* and Great Concentration.

It may be asked, "Why do copyists have to develop wisdom?"

The answer: Copyists of the Mahāyāna sutras must always utilize nonattachment, nonthought, and nondiscriminative wisdom. Further, they must elucidate these essential teachings: "*Saṃsāra* is *nirvāṇa*" and "Passions constitute Buddhahood." They must be able to calm and purify the heart and stop the waves of confused thinking from churning. One must transcend all opposition and advance toward the heart of things while avoiding acceptance or rejection of objects along the way. This is the immovable Diamond Wisdom and the door to [the teaching that] "All is mind alone."

It is a great joy to be mindful of the world's emptiness each moment yet not be separated from great compassion. It is a delight to be engaged in a thousand affairs yet not be ruled by emotion because the heart of emptiness is not forgotten.

In rest there is always action; in action there is always stillness. Action and stillness are two complementary wheels; mind

and meditation are the two feet and wings [of Buddhism]. Board
the Great White Cart of salvation and pass along the right road of
the Mahāyāna; abandon the little vehicles and cast off make-shift
theories.

Vow to attain all these principles and achieve the sixth level
of wisdom; always keep striving for a higher level. Maintain these
admonitions in your heart and there will be great happiness, great
happiness. Those who read, chant, study, explain, and preserve
the sutras should observe similar methods. Accrue virtue, encompass all things, and strive for the completion of the Buddhist Way
by yourself and by all sentient beings.

Saichō's reputation for learning and experience in meditation began to attract
other monks to Hiei, and plans were laid to establish a permanent monastery on the
mountain. Ichijō Shikan-in ("Cloister of Meditation on the One Vehicle") was
founded in 788. In it, Saichō enshrined an image of Yakushi Nyorai, the Buddha of
Healing, which he carved himself from a trunk of a fragrant sandalwood tree, to
remind him and his followers of their duty to help cure the ailments, spiritual and
physical, that plague the world. At the same time, Saichō kindled the "eternal flame
of the Dharma" before the image, a fire that still burns today. Other buildings
gradually went up, and Ichijō Shikan-in grew into a full-fledged monastic complex.
A dedication ceremony for the new monastery was held in 794, with representatives
from the main Nara schools and, according to some accounts, Emperor Kammu and
several of his senior advisors in attendance.

Following the Dōkyō debacle, Emperor Kōnin (709–782) instituted a series
of reforms aimed at curbing the power of the Nara temples and restoring Buddhism
to a pristine state. He insisted, for example, that priests and nuns be required to
understand the meaning of the texts they were chanting. Kōnin's successor, Kammu
(737–806), carried on the reforms, eventually deciding it best to abandon Nara and
its troublesome priests altogether and shift the capital elsewhere. A preliminary
move to Nagaoka failed for a variety of reasons, and, according to legend, Kammu
went to survey another site.

"This seems to be an auspicious place," Kammu remarked to his ministers.
"To the east is the Kamo River, an abode of the Blue Dragon. To the west is a great
plain for the White Tiger to roam. To the south there is a basin for the Red Phoenix

to dwell, and to the north are hills for the Black Reptile. This site has only one drawback—that large mountain to the northwest. That direction is the demon gate from which evil enters a city, and that mountain looks too forbidding."

"Rest assured," his ministers replied. "On that peak is a saintly priest named Saichō, leader of a dedicated group of monks who chant sutras and meditate day and night for the peace and enlightenment of the nation. Surely the prayers of Saichō and his followers will protect the new capital."

Kammu went ahead and established his court at Heiankyō (present-day Kyoto) and became a staunch supporter of Saichō. In 797, Kammu appointed Saichō one of the nation's ten "imperial monks" and decreed that Hiei be supported by public funds from taxes collected in Saichō's home province of Ōmi.

In 801 Saichō sponsored a ten-day lecture on Lotus Buddhism on Hiei, inviting representatives from the Nara schools to participate. The following year Saichō himself presented a series of lectures on the same theme at Takaosan-ji in the capital, leaving Hiei for the first time in seventeen years. Saichō's fresh interpretations of Buddhism were received with great acclaim, and Kammu offered to formally recognize Saichō's monastery as an independent school. Saichō, however, was concerned that his understanding of Tendai was not complete; since he had not studied under a Chinese Tendai master he could not be certain that the texts he was using were totally accurate. When he expressed the desire to visit China and study further, Kammu agreed to support him, saying, "Perfect your understanding of Tendai and all the other schools, and come back to establish the best form of Buddhism for this country." Arrangements were made for Saichō to join the upcoming imperial mission to China and to study there for one year. The customary stay for priests was generally longer, but the frail emperor did not want his favorite priest to be gone too long.

The trip to China in those days was perilous in the extreme—only one out of eleven missions dispatched during this period returned to Japan with crew and cargo intact, and hundreds perished at sea. Japanese shipwrights had yet to master the art of boatbuilding in that era, and their crafts had a disastrous tendency to split apart in rough seas. In April of 803 the mission set out from Naniwa (present-day Ōsaka) to Kyūshū in southern Japan, but one of the boats was crippled in a storm and forced back to port. Saichō and his party made it safely to Kyūshū, but they had to postpone their departure for the mainland until the other ship was repaired. Saichō spent his layover of one year and three months in Kyūshū studying, lecturing on the sutras, and carving images of Yakushi Nyorai for each of the four ships that would be attempting the voyage.

In July of 804 the four ships departed for China from Kyūshū. The chief envoy and his second-in-command were on the first ship together with a young monk named Kūkai, who had been admitted to the mission at the last minute; on the second ship were the other high-ranking officials, and Saichō accompanied by the translator-monk Gishin and one other attendant; on the third ship were scribes, accountants, and mission secretaries; the fourth ship contained shipwrights, translators, and dock hands.

Not long out of port, the party was hit by high winds and heavy seas. Ships one and two drifted apart in different directions toward the mainland; ship three was blown back to Kyūshū, and ship four was never heard from again. After fifty-four days at sea—Saichō chanted sutras and meditated ceaselessly in hopes of safeguarding the crew of thirty-seven—ship number two miraculously arrived at Ning-po, a port not far from Saichō's intended destination of T'ien-t'ai. (Ship number one had landed some twenty days earlier considerably to the south.)

After a brief period of recuperation in Ning-po, Saichō and his small party proceeded to Tai Province. There he was warmly received by the local prefect, a scholar bureaucrat with a keen interest in T'ien-t'ai Buddhism. The prefect fraternally accepted Saichō's gifts of a Japanese sword, paper, inks, and brushes, but he would not take any gold from the monks; in fact, he paid for the copying of T'ien-t'ai texts for Saichō out of his own funds. Fortuitously, the T'ien-t'ai Patriarch Tao-sui was lecturing at a temple in the provincial capital; Saichō was introduced to the master and studied with him for the duration of that stay. Tao-sui was the abbot of Hsui-ch'an Temple, located on the top of T'ien-t'ai on the site of Chih-i's original hermitage. That temple was a center of practice. At the base of Mount T'ien-t'ai was the much larger K'uo-ch'ing Temple, the setting for major ceremonies, ordinations, and public lectures. The abbot there was Hsing-man (d. 823), whom Saichō met when he finally visited the mountain. Both Patriarchs were delighted with Saichō, having been alerted in dreams to expect a monk from the east who would carry T'ien-t'ai teachings back across the ocean.

Actually, Saichō only spent about thirty days on T'ien-t'ai proper. He worshiped at the holy sites on the mountain, donated several sutras written in gold ink as a present from the Japanese emperor, distributed crystal rosaries as gifts to the monks, and asked Chinese Tien-t'ai scholars their opinion of *Lectures on the Lo-*

tus Teachings, a collection of notes made from the meeting sponsored by Saichō on Hiei in 801.

Also on Mount T'ien-t'ai Saichō had the opportunity to experience Niu-t'ou ("Ox-head") style Zen with the master Hsiu-jan, who headed one of the smaller temples on the mountain.

Niu-t'ou (Jap. Gozu, 594–657) was a lively eccentric typical of the early Zen masters. He preferred living in caves to temples and was on good terms with the birds, tigers, wolves, and other wild beasts that surrounded his hideouts. On the infrequent occasions that he did venture to a city to give a Dharma talk, he attracted thousands of listeners, and there were sometimes earthquakes during his discourses. Niu-t'ou is the subject of this well-known koan:

> Prior to meeting the Fourth Patriarch, birds brought Niu-t'ou food
> and flowers. Why? After meeting the Patriarch, the birds stopped
> doing so. Why?"[16]

Niu-t'ou's descendants tended to follow the master's example by living outdoors in wild and remote places and practicing "sky burial"—exposing dead bodies to the elements and animals of prey. One prominent member of the Niu-t'ou lineage was Tao-lin, "The Bird Nest Zen Master," who was active around the time Saichō was in China. Once Tao-lin was visited by the renowned poet Po Chu-i, who at the time was serving as prefect in the district.

"You are in a dangerous place," Po Chu-i said to the monk, who was perched high among the trees.

"You are in a far more dangerous one!" Tao-lin retorted.

"What is so dangerous about my position?" Po Chu-i wondered.

"You don't think that it is dangerous to be attacked by the passions and to be continually troubled by this and that?" Tao-lin told him.

Changing the subject, Po Chu-i asked, "What is the essence of Buddhism?"

Tao-lin shot back, "Not to commit evil, to perform all good, and to purify the mind: that is the teaching of all the Buddhas."

"Even a child of three knows that," the prefect-poet huffed.

"Yes, but even a man of eighty cannot do it!" Tao-lin countered.

Such Zenlike detachment high above the world appealed to Saichō, and he studied Niu-t'ou teachings with deep interest.

Saichō accompanied Tao-sui back to the capital (where the abbot was actually based) and trained with the T'ien-t'ai master for four and a half months. During this second stay in the provincial capital, Saichō received the Bodhisattva precepts from Tao-sui as well as a formal certificate of transmission of the T'ien-t'ai teachings. Loaded down with texts, Saichō hired four extra porters to help carry the baggage. His stated goal thus fulfilled, Saichō prepared to return to Japan. Upon arrival in Ning-po, however, he discovered that the return trip to Japan was to be delayed for another month or two. The industrious Saichō characteristically made good use of the unexpected free time by seeking out the priest Shun-hsiao, a master of esoteric science who taught in a nearby province. Saichō received various initiations from that teacher and further augmented his supply of texts.

Thus, during his brief nine-month stay in China, the determined Saichō achieved proficiency in the four pillars of Mahāyāna Buddhism: T'ien-t'ai philosophy, Zen meditation, Bodhisattva precepts, and esoteric teachings.

Saichō returned safely to Japan in the summer of 805 with a rich collection of texts, some 460 volumes in all, on Tendai, Zen, Shingon, Pure Land, and Precept Buddhism; Taoist teachings; and other miscellaneous works plus ritual instruments and a variety of tea seedlings, herbs, and plants from the continent. Upon his return to Hiei, Saichō embarked on a second period of intense training, day and night poring over the texts that he had brought back with him, sorting out the esoteric initiations he had received, and meditating on his experiences with the Chinese masters.

Sixty-year-old Emperor Kammu, in precarious health and likely hoping for a miracle cure, implored Saichō to conduct an esoteric initiation ceremony for the court, and Saichō obliged in the fall of that year. The following January two monks from Hiei were registered as "national ordinands" and Saichō's Tendai Hokke School received formal status as an independent sect.

In the meantime, the young monk Kūkai had also returned to Japan after receiving the full transmission—in precipitously short time—of esoteric Shingon (Chin. Chen-yen) from the Chinese master Hui-kuo (746–805). Ever-eager to supplement his knowledge and pursue a deeper understanding of the truth, Saichō borrowed a number of texts from Kūkai. Realizing that his own initiation into esotericism was still rudimentary, Saichō unhesitatingly requested a higher-level initiation from Kūkai, which he received at a special ceremony held in Takaosan-ji at the end of 812.

However, in 813 Kūkai refused Saichō's request to borrow a commentary on an important esoteric text, explaining rather arrogantly that esoteric teachings must be transmitted from mind to mind and that mere copying was not enough to achieve true understanding. As Kūkai put it: "Words are rubble; the profundities of the secret doctrines are not found in the sentences of a text." In other words, Kūkai was demanding that Saichō become a full-fledged follower of Shingon and admit that Tendai teaching was inferior, something that Saichō—who knew quite well that texts were nothing more than roadmaps—was not willing to do.

A break between the two great Patriarchs was inevitable. Saichō, seven years Kūkai's senior and of higher social rank, was idealistic, introspective, stern, and reserved; Kūkai, by contrast, was charismatic, ambitious, supremely confident, outgoing, and shrewd. Saichō was certainly Kūkai's intellectual equal, but his austere and self-effacing character made him a less appealing figure than the lively and charming Kūkai. (One modern commentator has described the difference between the two Patriarchs in these terms: "Saichō is the type of person you would ask for help with your homework; Kūkai is the fellow you would invite to a class party to stir things up.")

For the flamboyant Kūkai, Shingon was the ultimate; for the abstemious Saichō, esoteric Buddhism enhanced but did not supersede Tendai. A further blow to the relationship was the defection to Kūkai of Saichō's top disciple and designated successor, Taihan. Taihan refused to return to Hiei despite repeated entreaties by the forlorn Saichō, and in 816 Kūkai went so far as to pen a reply in Taihan's name delineating the reasons for the switch in loyalties. That effectively severed the relationship between the Shingon master and the Tendai teacher.

(Even after their deaths, Kūkai continued to far outshine Saichō. Deified as Kōbō Daishi (the "Great Master Who Spread the Dharma"), Kūkai became Japan's most popular saint, an artist, thinker, and wonder-worker of unimaginable proportions, while appreciation for the dignified Saichō was confined to Tendai circles. In recent years, though, Saichō's stock has risen quite a bit, especially among Japanese and foreign scholars. Kūkai is undeniably a folk hero, but his overwhelming presence so dominates Shingon that there is simply no other monk in that tradition who comes close to rivaling the master. Saichō's eclectic Tendai, on the contrary, has spawned an unbroken line of outstanding priests who have shaped Japanese Buddhism. In terms of actual influence on the development of Buddhism in Japan, the Tendai Patriarch is the dominant figure and Saichō's Hiei is clearly superior to

Kūkai's Kōya as a center of Buddhist study and practice.)[17]

Saichō traveled widely between the years 814 and 818, visiting distant Kyūshū and eastern Japan to teach, dedicate images he had carved, and distribute copies of the *Lotus Sūtra*. In 818, during a drought, Saichō's successful rainmaking ceremony considerably enhanced his reputation.

During the same period, Saichō was conducting a debate, via religious tracts, with the Kegon scholar Tokuitsu. The debate was highly technical but in essence the dispute centered on Tokuitsu's claim that the One Vehicle of the *Lotus Sūtra* was a provisional teaching, while the Three Vehicle doctrine of Kegon was the ultimate; further, enlightenment could only be won by certain worthy individuals after many lifetimes of training. Saichō rejected that notion, arguing, as stated in the *Lotus Sūtra,* that all beings are capable of attaining enlightenment in this very body. As proof, Saichō cited the story of the eight-year-old water maiden—the lowest of the low—being transformed into a Bodhisattva through the power of the *Lotus Sūtra* (chapter 12).

There is a tale, almost certainly apocryphal, that Tokuitsu came to Hiei once to see Saichō. The Tendai master politely went to greet the Kegon scholar at the base of the mountain. There Tokuitsu noticed a sickly pear tree that had not borne any fruit.

"Even on this holy mountain, where it is said that grasses and trees become Buddha, there is a barren fruit tree," Tokuitsu challenged Saichō.

Saichō calmly replied, "Do you not know that on this mountain where even grasses and trees become Buddha, there is nourishing water everywhere?" He thereupon chanted a *mantra,* struck a rock beneath the tree, and spring water bubbled up to feed it.[18]

Saichō was confident that his Tendai teaching was the most complete and adaptable but realized that without an independent base his school would never survive. For some years he longed to establish an ordination platform on Hiei, for both theoretical and practical reasons. If the Tendai school could conduct its own ordinations, its future would be secure.

Although Saichō had faithfully observed the full monastic rule which he had received at age nineteen, he considered the Hīnayāna precepts to be outmoded and too impractical to implement. Saichō urged the replacement of the old rules with the Bodhisattva precepts, which are based on the spirit rather than the letter of Buddhism. The Bodhisattva precepts consist of the following.[19]

THE TEN CARDINAL PRECEPTS

Not to:

1. Deprive any being of life
2. Steal or misuse any material
3. Indulge in illicit sex
4. Speak falsehood or act unjustly
5. Deal in intoxicants
6. Find fault with others
7. Boast about oneself in front of others
8. Begrudge requests for help and ignore the pleas of those in need
9. Become angry and despise others
10. Dishonor the Three Treasures

THE FORTY-EIGHT MINOR PRECEPTS

To refrain from:

1. Disrespect toward others
2. Drinking liquor
3. Eating raw flesh
4. Eating spicy (i.e., sexually stimulating) food
5. Not counseling or encouraging others to keep the precepts
6. Inhospitality
7. Inattention to the Dharma
8. Preferring non-Buddhist teachings to the Mahāyāna
9. Ignoring the sick and needy
10. Possessing weapons
11. Inciting war or joining an army
12. Trading in slaves, animals, and dead bodies
13. Speaking unkindly of others
14. Ravaging nature
15. Teaching non-Buddhist doctrines
16. Associating with the rich and powerful
17. Defrauding the poor and weak
18. Instructing with insufficient knowledge of the Dharma
19. Creating dissension

20. Not liberating suffering beings
21. Exacting revenge
22. Excessive pride in one's attainments
23. Not giving instruction because of indolence, corruption, or arrogance
24. Inadequate devotion to the Three Treasures
25. Misappropriation and waste
26. Misuse of hospitality on one's behalf
27. Accepting personal favors
28. Favoring some person or group over others
29. Inappropriate occupations (prostitution, fortune-telling, sorcery, etc.)
30. Not observing holy days and months
31. Not preventing Buddha images from being bought and sold by non-Buddhists
32. Conducting fraudulent business transactions
33. Watching violent sports, seeing plays, or listening to lewd music
34. Being separated from the Bodhi-mind
35. Not fostering a mind for the Dharma
36. Laxity toward the precepts
37. Disregarding the rules for periods of intense training
38. Nonobservance of the established order
39. Neglect of proclaiming the Dharma and caring for those in distress
40. Considering social status when ordaining novices
41. Teaching for selfish or pernicious reasons
42. Teaching before an unsuitable crowd of nonbelievers
43. Accepting donations while not observing the precepts
44. Disrespect for the sutras
45. Forgetting the vow to retain great compassion and lead all to enlightenment
46. Not proclaiming the Dharma properly
47. Formulating laws contrary to Buddhism
48. Subordinating Buddhism through unjust laws

In addition to his philosophical opposition to the old Hīnayāna precepts, Saichō was highly reluctant to send his disciples to Nara for ordination. Of the twenty Tendai trainees ordained as government-sponsored monks between 807 and 817, only six returned to Hiei, the monastery known for four things—incessant study, high humidity, freezing cold, and poverty. A few were unable to continue for reasons of health, but most of the young monks found the attractions of Nara—a temperate climate, magnificent, well-supplied temples, and well-heeled patrons—too much to resist.

Consequently, in 818, Saichō discarded the precepts he had followed for thirty years and publicly announced his adherence to the Bodhisattva rules. In 818, Saichō submitted to the court his "Regulations for Student Monks of the Mountain Monastery" (*Sange-gakusho-shiki*),[20] setting forth his views on the question of the precepts and requesting imperial sanction to construct an ordination platform on Hiei. Emperor Saga (786–842) was at the time under Kūkai's influence and referred the matter to the Priests Council in Nara, which was naturally vehemently opposed to this direct challenge to their power. The council urged the emperor to dismiss Saichō's petition; the original precepts had been formualted by Śākyamuni himself, and an upstart such as Saichō should not be allowed to tamper with the system. Furthermore, they said, Saichō lacked the necessary credentials to head up his own independent school, for his stay in China was of insufficient duration.

Saichō defended his views in *Clarification of the Precepts (Kenkairon)*, issued in 820, but the years of asceticism and the long struggle to establish Tendai took its toll, and in 822, the fifty-six-year-old Patriarch fell gravely ill. In his final days, Saichō gave various injunctions to his disciples: "The worthless Saichō, tired from all his labors, has exhausted his life. . . . I will be gone soon, and I have done only two things of merit: never letting harsh words pass my lips nor allowing my hands to injure a living being. . . . Do not build images or write sutras in my memory— just make my intentions known." Saichō also counseled his charges not to get involved in worldly affairs, not to construct fancy buildings or monastic estates, and to strictly avoid wine and women during the course of their training. "Practice Buddha-like perfection and compassion, remain true to the One Vehicle and its wisdom. Make great efforts! Make great efforts!"

Saichō died on the twenty-second day of the sixth month of 822. A week later the remorseful Saga dispatched a messenger to Hiei carrying permission to build an ordination platform, together with a poem lamenting the death of the Tendai Patriarch.

Beneath the towering trees the noble monk who strove
    to elucidate and transmit the Tendai teachings
Now lies still, his work completed.
A new tomb has been dug in the earth
Where he shall dwell forever, surrounded by pines.
The light of the Dharma illuminates the Master's empty
    room and incense smoke swirls around the Buddha
    images he carved;
Few will ever approach his level and keep the
    precepts as faithfully as he did.
The Master has departed from this world
And nothing can assuage my grief at his death.[21]

In 837, Saichō's dream came true with the completion of the construction of an ordination platform on Hiei. In 886, the court declared him Dengyō Daishi, "The Great Teacher Who Transmitted the Dharma."

Saichō's Tendai was far more than a Japanese version of the Chinese T'ien-t'ai. T'ien-t'ai philosophy was at the base of Tendai, but the humble Saichō, willing to learn from everything and anyone, also freely incorporated other elements into his system, including the indigenous Shintō.[22] Saichō was a grand synthesizer who made room, somewhere, for everything in the Tendai edifice. The Patriarch valued Zen meditation, passive and active, as an expression of the truth of emptiness and at the same time appreciated Tantric esotericism—with its visualizations, incantations, icons, rituals, and imagery—as a valid method of functioning in the relative world of name and form. His Tendai, Saichō hoped, would be the integrator that balanced the two realities and, further, illuminated all other religious practices by displaying their essential unity. In short, "Great unity, insignificant differences."

Although, as we shall see later, esotericism temporarily gained the upper hand on Hiei, thus briefly destroying the balance of Tendai, Saichō's balanced eclecticism eventually prevailed, and today the Patriarch's Lotus Buddhism of the One Vehicle is once again the guiding light of Hiei.

THE MAGIC
MOUNTAIN
The History of Hiei [1]

ALTHOUGH SAICHŌ had numerous followers nationwide at the time of his rather forlorn death, the monastery on Hiei consisted of a few modest buildings, a handful of monks, and a small group of lay brothers. In time, however, Enryaku-ji—the new name bestowed on the mountain monastery by Emperor Saga in 823—grew into one of the largest religious complexes the world has ever seen, a virtual state within itself, peopled by some of the best—and worst—Buddhist priests of all time. Throughout its long and varied history, Tendai Buddhism has encompassed the lofty and the base, the sacred and the profane, the sublime and the awful.

Despite Saichō's deathbed plea to his disciples to treat each other with compassion when he was no longer there to guide them, there was trouble almost immediately after the Patriarch's demise. In accordance with Saichō's final instructions, Gishin (780–833)—the senior disciple, who accompanied the master to China as interpreter—assumed the position of *zasu* (abbot) of Enryaku-ji and head of the Tendai sect. When Gishin died in 833, two monks claimed the right to be named the new *zasu:* Gishin's disciple Enshū (n.d.) and Enchō (771–837), another of Saichō's designated Dharma heirs. When the court ruled in favor of Enchō, the disgruntled Enshū left Hiei in a huff and settled in Muro-ji with a group of supporters. When Enchō died two and a half years later, the dispute resumed. For the next eighteen years the position of abbot was left vacant and Enryaku-ji's affairs were conducted by an administrator and a triumvirate council of monks. It was not until 854 that a suitable candidate was found.

The third Tendai *zasu* was Ennin (Jikaku Daishi, 794–864).[2] Ennin was ordained a novice monk at age nine, and around the age of fifteen he dreamt one night of encountering a great cleric. Upon being informed by his seniors that the saint he was describing must be Saichō, Ennin immediately set off for Hiei. Ennin became one of Saichō's closest disciples; following the master's death, he began lecturing widely on the *Lotus Sūtra*. Ennin suddenly fell gravely ill, however, and returned to Hiei to prepare for the end. After several years of seclusion in a hermitage, Ennin miraculously recovered his full strength, and in 834 he was nominated by his Tendai superiors to be a member of the latest (and last, it turned out, for several centuries) embassy to China. Once again, Saichō appeared to Ennin in a dream, urging the young monk "to complete my work in China." Even though thirty years had passed since the previous mission in 805, the trip was not any safer than before. The first two attempts were aborted in 836 and 837, and the third launching in 838 was just barely successful, Ennin's party reaching the mainland only after a shipwreck off the Chinese coast.

Ennin, to his great dismay, was prevented from going to T'ien-t'ai by suspicious Chinese bureaucrats, who ordered the monk to return to Japan on the next boat. Undeterred, Ennin, with the connivance of Korean monks and merchants he had befriended, surreptitiously remained in the country, eventually making his way to the two main Buddhist centers of Wu-t'ai and Ch'ang-an to study. Ennin survived the harsh persecution of Buddhism by the crazed Emperor Wu-tsing and, after many adventures, returned safely to Japan, loaded down with texts, after a nine-and-a-half-year stay on the mainland.

In addition to his treasure trove of Buddhist books, Ennin carried back with him a profound knowledge of esoteric Buddhism. (He reportedly was less enthusiastic about Zen, being somewhat nonplussed by the wild behavior of the Ch'an monks he encountered in China.) Unlike Saichō, Ennin had the time to master the complete Tantric system of the Diamond World (*vajradhātu*), the Womb World (*garbhadhātu*), and the Integrated World (*susiddhi*). The Diamond World represents the adamantine wisdom that cuts through all illusion; the Womb World stands for the potentiality of enlightenment, the seeds to be germinated. When the two worlds are integrated, incredible energy is generated, resulting in the "miraculous powers" seemingly manifested by awakened beings.

Ennin's knowledge of Tantric rites made him immensely popular with the ever-superstitious members of the imperial court; the emperor and most of his ministers received the Bodhisattva precepts from him. Ennin was indeed a great magician. He once became possessed by the god of sickness, tamed it, and then created a talisman to ward off plague that is still used by people of Kyoto to protect themselves from illness and disease.

Ennin's Tantric system was further refined and expanded by the priests on Hiei, and Tendai esotericism—known as *Taimitsu* to distinguish it from the *Tōmitsu* of Shingon—became so popular in this period that a few monks such as Annen (d. 902) advocated changing the name of the school to Shingon and replacing the *Lotus Sūtra* with the *Dainichi-kyō (Mahāvairocana-sūtra)*, the main Tantric text. Generally speaking, Tendai esotericism tends to be more devotional, rational, and philosophical than Shingon, with its emphasis on empowerment, paradox, and ideation.[3]

In addition to a complete Tantric system, Ennin also introduced, based on his experiences on Wu-t'ai, the practices of Chanting the Name of Amida Buddha (*nembutsu*) and mountain pilgrimage (*kaihōgyō*) to Hiei. As Abbot, he oversaw the further development of the original complex and supervised the opening up of the Yokawa district. Although Ennin gave specific instructions not to enshrine his body—"Only Saichō should have a mausoleum on this mountain"—he is often spoken of as the Co-Founder of Tendai.

The other main figure of early Tendai was Enchin (Chishō Daishi, 814–891), the fifth *zasu*. Enchin, too, studied in China, remaining there for five years; unlike Ennin, Enchin was able to make it to Mount T'ien-t'ai (where, incidentally, he rebuilt a small temple for Japanese student monks that had originally been established by Saichō). Enchin returned to Japan in 858 with one thousand Buddhist texts. An acknowledged master of esotericism, Enchin served as *zasu* for twenty-three years, overseeing the construction of hundreds of buildings on Hiei itself and the establishment of a large complex at Onjō-ji (Mii-dera) as his personal power base.

Following Enchin's death an irreparable breach occurred between the so-called Saichō-Ennin line and the Gishin-Enchin line of Japanese Tendai. Although Gishin had accompanied Saichō to China (he actually received some initiations that his

In Tendai Buddhism, even trees, stones, and ponds have the potential to become Buddhas. Here a marathon monk salutes a sacred tree. ▶

master did not) and was expressly designated by Saichō as his successor, Gishin had spent much of his career after returning from the mainland away from Hiei and had few disciples or supporters there. Gishin's relationship with Saichō's later disciples (and perhaps even with Saichō himself) was strained, and an "anti-Gishin" faction evolved. This group considered Ennin, not Gishin, to be the true heir of Saichō; indeed, as mentioned above, they thought of Ennin as the second "founder" of Japanese Tendai and bitterly opposed the innovations of Enchin, who was in the Gishin lineage.

Many grave problems also arose due to the organizational structure of the monasteries on Hiei. Since the mountain's new subtemples were founded and funded by members of the imperial family and other aristocrats, securing influential and rich patrons became the primary object of a majority of temples. This is one of the reasons that worldly esotericism was so popular in the early history of Tendai— each temple devised its own secret rites and boasted of its power to attract super-stitious supporters. Temples that did obtain such backing became quite wealthy. Saichō's heartfelt admonition, "Set your mind on the Way and clothing and food will be there,"[4] was completely forgotten; temples began to conduct trade and establish commercial concerns to increase the size of their treasuries. Each large temple functioned as a more or less independent entity and engaged large numbers of assistant priests (*dōnin*) and lay brothers (*kunin*) to maintain and protect their establishment. Attracted by the promise of free food and lodging, the ranks of temple aides and lay workers were rapidly infiltrated by vagabonds, brigands, and eventually mercenaries. Contrary to Saichō's strict injunctions, horses, cattle, and weapons were provisioned on Hiei, and each monastic faction on the mountain organized its own militia, justifying such armed forces as an absolute necessity to protect Buddhism from its "enemies" in these degenerate "Last Days of the Dharma." As each faction strove to improve its fortunes and consolidate its position, conflicts arose between rival gangs and attacks and violent reprisals became common-place. Buildings were constantly being torched, and the entire mountain turned into one large armed camp.

Ryōgen (Jie Daishi, 913–986), the eighteenth Tendai *zasu,* attempted to put an end to the terrible abuses on the mountain. He succeeded in restoring the buildings that had been destroyed by arson and in reorganizing the monastic educational system, but he failed miserably to curb the power of the dreaded *sōhei,*

◄ Kompon Chū-dō, main temple of the vast Enryaku-ji complex of Hiei.

[33]

"warrior-monks," who now dominated the mountain.[5] A telling passage in Ryōgen's biography relates how, as a young monk, he longed to escape the pollution of Hiei and seek refuge as a lay hermit in the distant mountains—for true men of the Way had virtually disappeared from Tendai monasteries. Ryōgen was another *zasu* who did not want a mausoleum built for him: "Leave my grave to the natural elements and let me return to the original state of Suchness." A single stone (fronted by a large hall!) marks his resting place.

A few years after Ryōgen's death, Yokei, a member of the Gishin-Enchin line, was appointed *zasu* by imperial decree, but the monks of the Saichō-Ennin lineage refused to accept the appointment. When a delegation of imperial troops was dispatched to enforce the order, they were ambushed by a band of *sōhei* who tore the imperial edict into shreds and forced the troops back to the capital. The court later succeeded in having Yokei installed as *zasu,* but the opposition of half the mountain to his tenure made it impossible for him to govern the place, and he soon resigned the post. Civil war ensued; the Saichō-Ennin faction gained the upper hand, razing the temples of the Gishin-Enchin clique and driving the members of that group, perhaps a thousand in all, off Hiei. The defeated party ensconced themselves in the sanctuary of Onjō-ji at the base of Hiei; forever after there was a permanent split and continual skirmishing between the temples on Hiei (*sammon*) and the group based at Onjō-ji (*jimon*). In the ensuing centuries, Hiei became ever more powerful, emerging as an independent state waging war with a host of religious and secular foes.

The battles fought on Hiei itself were between the lower-ranking temple aides and lay workers (*dōshū*) and the more upper-class regular priests (*gakushō* or *gakutō*), almost all of them hailing from aristocratic families. (The abbot of a subtemple, known as *inge,* was invariably a widowed or homosexual nobleman who had retired from the world and taken Buddhist vows.) There were disputes over territorial claims, funds, selection of Tendai officials, even fights over who had precedence in bathing in monastic bathhouses. During the turbulent medieval period some of the *zasu* were in office only a day or two before being ousted by one faction or the other. Since the strength of the *dōshū* and the *gakushō* was roughly equal, about two thousand men on each side, there was a continual stalemate, neither party being able to gain permanent control of the mountain.

Off the mountain, the most hated enemies of the Hiei warrior-monks were the *jimon* priests of Onjō-ji; during the Middle Ages, Hiei *sōhei* reduced Onjō-ji to ashes nine times. The following tale gives an idea of the implacable hatred between the two Tendai factions.

The Onjō-ji priest Raigō was renowned for his miraculous powers, and the heirless emperor Shirakawa beseeched the Tantric master to pray for the birth of a crown prince. Raigō assented and, sure enough, the emperor's consort conceived and gave birth to a baby boy. When the grateful emperor asked the priest how he could be repaid, Raigō replied, "By granting permission for me to construct a Tendai ordination platform independent of Hiei." The emperor wanted to grant the wish but could not run the risk of retaliation by the *sōhei* of Hiei. Shirakawa—who once made the famous lament "There are three things in this world beyond the control of any man: the roll of the dice, the floodwaters of the Kamo River, and the monks of Hiei"—procrastinated as long as he could but then had to refuse to honor Raigō's request. The grim Raigō told the emperor, "You will regret your decision," and then secluded himself in a hall at Onjō-ji to cast a spell on the crown prince. Shirakawa's son never saw his fourth birthday. His diabolical mission accomplished, Raigō too died. Thereupon, Hiei was infested by a plague of rats, which viciously attacked the books, images, and buildings on the mountain. The Hiei monks were convinced that the plague was the work of Raigō's malevolent spirit and embarked on a furious bout of exorcism.

In addition to sweeps against Onjō-ji and the court in Kyoto, Hiei marauders took on the temple armies of Nara and ruthlessly attacked any new Buddhist sect that dared to attempt to establish itself—even though nearly all the leaders of those new schools were originally Hiei monks.

Ryōnin (1072–1132), founder of the Yūzū Nembutsu sect, entered Hiei at age twelve. After performing the 1,000-day mountain pilgrimage in Mudō-ji Valley, Ryōnin secluded himself in peaceful Ohara Valley, devoting his days to Tendai Pure Land teachings and melodic chanting of Amida Buddha's name. Following visions of Amida himself and the Indian *deva* Bishamonten (Vaiśravana), Ryōnin began to preach publicly and establish a new sect. His Yūzū ("inner-penetrating") Nembutsu was derived from Kegon and Tendai universalism—"One person equals all other persons; one practice equals all other practices"—particularized in a simple, rhythmic chant that anyone could perform. All elements of existence were incorporated in the chanting of Buddha's name, and by totally abandoning oneself to the practice, reciting the *nembutsu* hundreds or, if possible, thousands of times a day, one could bridge all opposition and distinctions—in other words, achieve unity with all things. Ryōnin escaped persecution from his Tendai brothers, but the other founders were not so lucky.

Hōnen (1133–1212), the founder of the Pure Land (*Jōdo*) school, became a monk on Hiei following the death of his samurai father in a night raid on the family home. Hōnen lived in the Kurodani section of Hiei for many years, practicing Tendai-style *nembutsu* and going through the entire Buddhist canon five times. Suddenly realizing that single-minded chanting of Amida Buddha's name was to be his Way, Hōnen decided to leave the mountain and teach in the marketplace.

After his move to Kyoto, Hōnen attracted thousands of followers and, not incidentally, the enmity of his former brother monks on Hiei, who bitterly persecuted the Pure Land Patriarch both during his own lifetime and after. Hiei bandits seized the printing blocks and as many existing copies of Hōnen's works as they could turn up and made a huge bonfire out of them in the Enryaku-ji courtyard. In 1227 Hiei terrorists were dispatched on a mission to rob Hōnen's grave and cast the corpse into the Kamo River (for some reason Hōnen had not been cremated at death). Imperial troops guarding the site thwarted the plot at the last minute.

Hōnen's chief disciple, Shinran, founder of the True Pure Land (*Jōdō Shinshū*) school, also spent nearly twenty years on Hiei engaging in *nembutsu* meditation and the mountain marathon. Legend states that Shinran collapsed on the last day of the 1,000-day marathon and hovered near death. Inspired by a vision he received in that trancelike state, Shinran departed from Hiei and, after many vicissitudes, brought the Jōdō Shinshū into being, later to become, numerically, the largest Buddhist sect in Japan. Shinran is said to have been deeply influenced by Saichō's sense of humility, and it has been suggested that Shinran's decision to marry and live as "neither priest, neither layman" was simply carrying Saichō's Tendai universalism a step further by bringing the Mahāyāna teaching within the reach of every person, high or low, male or female. Shinran himself spent much of his life away from the capital and thus avoided direct repression by the Hiei warrior-monks; his Hongan-ji headquarters was not spared Hiei's wrath, though, being burned to the ground by the *sōhei* in 1458.

Although Eisai (1146–1215) is venerated as the founder of Rinzai Zen in Japan, he remained, nominally, a Tendai priest all his life. Eisai was ordained on Hiei as a youth and immersed himself in Tendai esotericism. Sorely distressed by the corruption and internecine feuding of Japanese Buddhism, Eisai traveled twice to China (and entertained hopes of going as far as India) in search of the True Dharma. In China he spent considerable time on T'ien-t'ai and coincidentally received an *inka* (document of transmission) from a Chinese master of Huang-lung Ch'an certifying the Japanese priest as a teacher of Lin-chi (Jap. Rinzai) Zen. When Eisai attempted to introduce that form of Buddhism into Japan, the elders of Hiei naturally protested. Eisai was eventually able to open a meditation hall at Kennin-ji in Kyoto with the proviso that it be a branch temple of Hiei and that he concurrently continue Tendai practices.

The other Zen Patriarch, the aloof and austere Dōgen (1200–1253), began his monastic career on Hiei at age twelve. He was disgusted by the decadence of Hiei and the inability of Tendai doctors to answer this question: "Both the exoteric and esoteric schools teach that all beings possess Buddha-nature and original enlightenment. If that is so, why do all the Buddhas of the three worlds arouse the Bodhi-seeking mind and search for enlightenment through practice?"

Dōgen also made the long journey to China to find someone who could resolve his doubts. There he encountered the Patriarch Ju-ching (Jap. Nyōjō, 1163–1228), who invested him with transmission of the Ts'ao-tung (Jap. Sōtō) Zen lineage. Like Eisai, Dōgen's innovations alarmed the ever-suspicious Hiei clerics, and they resorted to their usual tactics: denunciations to the authorities and direct threats against Dōgen's person. The Sōtō Zen Patriarch had the good sense to accept an invitation to build a monastery in Echigō, hundreds of miles from the capital, and thus was able to teach and write without interference from the brigands of Hiei.

Nichiren (1222–1282), the founder of the aggressive sect that bears his name, likely acquired some of his fanaticism from a Hiei priest called Shunban, "The Grand Inquisitor" of Tendai. After training on Hiei for some years, Nichiren concluded that he alone was the true heir of Saichō and that it was his divine mission to restore the fortunes of the Lotus sect in Japan. Even though he later conceived of himself as an incarnation of the Buddha, Nichiren generously included the Tendai Patriarchs Chih-i and Saichō in the Nichiren pantheon of saints. The Hiei *sōhei* were not pacified by that gesture, and although they were briefly allied with the Nichiren sect against the Pure Land schools, they turned on their former comrades-in-arms and burned every one of that sect's temples in Kyoto to the ground, in the process slaughtering every Nichiren adherent they could lay their hands on. The Nichiren sect in Kyoto never recovered from that blow.

Ippen (1239–1289), the last of the great founders to have studied Tendai, began his career on Hiei as a novice monk around the age of ten. In true Tendai eclectic style, Ippen went on to train at the sacred Shintō mountain of Kumano, at the Shingon *maṇḍala* peak of Kōya, and at most of the other holy spots in the country before settling on the "dancing *nembutsu*" as his primary method of impart-

ing Buddhism to the masses. Ippen's teaching, the foundation of the Ji ("Time")
sect, aroused the disapproval of Tendai prelates, but the diplomatic master—he had
received certification from both Zen *and* Nichiren teachers—avoided a direct con-
frontation by spending his final years in distant Shikoku, his birthplace.

It is said that those who live by the sword shall perish by the sword, and by the
middle of the fifteenth century, the internal corruption of Hiei—Saichō's mountain,
the first training site in Japan to have banned alcohol and all sexual activity, was now
overrun with drunkards, sodomites, rapists, and whores—had fatally rotted the
pillars of the mountain fortress. In 1433 the warriors of Onjō-ji were, for the first
time, successful in repelling an all-out attack by Hiei *sōhei,* and the newly ascendant
Ashikaga Shogunate made inroads on Enryaku-ji's power, taking over places previously under Hiei's domain. The rumor formerly spread by Hiei clerics that the
killing of a priest would cause one's family to be plagued for seven generations was
now laughed at, and the old ploy of marching behind a sacred palanquin to
discourage retaliation no longer worked.

Enryaku-ji's days were really numbered when it foolishly sided against the
ruthless warlord Oda Nobunaga (1534–1582). Nobunaga would stop at nothing in
his drive to bring all of Japan under his rule, and he was cowed neither by the threat
of Hiei's curses nor by its arsenal:

> If I do not take them away now, this great trouble will be everlast-
> ing. Moreover, those priests violate their vows: they eat fish and
> stinking vegetables, keep concubines and never unroll the sacred
> books. How can they be vigilant against evil, or maintain the
> right? Surround their dens and burn them, and suffer none of them
> within to live![6]

In 1571, a battalion of 25,000 troops unleashed a furious assault on the
mountain fortress, torching all the buildings and massacring the inmates. The
conflagration—perhaps not an unwelcome sight for the countless victims of *sōhei*
terrorism—lit up the sky for three days and nights and the ashes of some three
thousand temples blanketed the capital.[7]

Later, the violent Nobunaga himself suffered karmic retribution—he was
assassinated by his enemies in 1582. The families that succeeded Nobunaga as
leaders of the country, the Toyotomi and the Tokugawa, were in favor of restoring

Hiei—who knew what mischief the vengeful spirits of the monks might create—but, not surprisingly, on a much smaller and safer scale: no more than a twentieth of its former size and under direct control of the Shogunate. Between 1585 and 1650, temples arose, phoenixlike, from the ashes on Hiei and the mountain gradually assumed the form we see today.

The Tokugawa Shoguns rigidly controlled society for the next two and a half centuries, closing the country off from the outside world and strictly regulating every aspect of life. Buddhist temples were turned into showplaces, registry offices, and funeral homes. All was peaceful, a welcome state after centuries of warfare, but during the Tokugawa period Buddhism stagnated. One Hiei monk, named Myōryū (1637–1690), went so far as to abandon the Mahāyāna precepts in favor of the original Hīnayāna rules to protest the secularization of Tendai priests. Myōryū contended that Hiei monks were too much like civil servants (which in fact was what most Buddhist priests were in those days) and Confucian functionaries. In order to restore Buddhism to Hiei, Myōryū proposed strict observance of the original monastic precepts. Outraged by this apparent insult to the memory of Saichō, who had devoted his career to establishing the Mahāyāna precepts in Japan, the other monks chased him off the mountain. In typical Tendai fashion, however, Myōryū was later allowed to found a small precepts temple at the base of Hiei and permitted to follow the ancient monastic rule as Saichō himself had once done, thereby contributing to the correct understanding of the Mahāyāna!

The forced opening of Japan to foreign trade in the 1850s and the Meiji Restoration of 1868 drastically affected Buddhism. It was disestablished in favor of State Shintō, and its creed was ridiculed by Shintō nationalists, Christian missionaries, and Westernized intellectuals. Although actual persecution was mild (there was some burning of Buddhist material at the base of Hiei in the early days of Meiji), Buddhism was definitely on the defensive, and Hiei, like all the other Buddhist schools, experienced hard times right up until the renaissance of the present day—brought about largely by the marathon monks.

STUDY AND PRACTICE

The Way of Tendai Buddhism [1]

IN India, Vulture Peak; in China, T'ien-t'ai; in Japan, Hiei. On those sacred mountains of the East, the Lotus Teaching of the Good Law has been proclaimed, in myriad tongues and in all manner of ways, throughout the ages in hope of bringing complete and perfect enlightenment to all beings whatever their circumstance.

Of the three, Hiei is the only one that remains easily accessible. As mentioned above, the mountain has been the focal point of Buddhism in Japan; all the major schools either developed in conjunction with or directly from Tendai. Hiei continues to retain a particular fascination, for it offers the seeker every type of religious experience—sacred scholarship, grand ritual, austere meditation, heartfelt repentance, heroic asceticism, mystical flight, miraculous cures, ceaseless devotion, divine joy, and nature worship—while promising enlightenment in this very body. Further, it provides the seeker with a splendid environment—stately buildings, sumptuous Buddha Halls, icons of celestial beauty, music from heaven, food and drink seemingly prepared by the gods, magic costumes, spectacular scenery and breathtaking views—to support the seeker in his or her quest. This is as Saichō intended: "Even with the best of intentions it is difficult to master the Way under unfavorable conditions; living in a quiet place in the bosom of nature is the most conducive for practice. It is better to rely, at first, on the place rather than the mind."[2] Superstition, ignorance, greed, covetousness, and all the other human follies are ever-present, too, on Hiei, but that is the way Buddhism functions in the world—it never exists in a vacuum but right in the midst of *saṃsāra,* which is, according to the first principle of Buddha, forever imperfect.

The grand spectacle that is Tendai Buddhism is symbolized by the "Eternal Flame of the Dharma" first kindled by Saichō 1,200 years ago. As an idealistic young monk, Saichō ignited the spark in front of his hand-carved image of Yakushi Nyorai, housed in a flimsy little hut, firm in his belief that it would burn forever.

Later, he added to the flame some of the brilliance he had carried back with him from T'ien-t'ai in China. Evildoers on the mountain caused the flame to be temporarily snuffed out when corrupt Tendai priests suffered the consequences of perverting Buddhism, but other pure practitioners protected the light in distant temples. When Hiei was rebuilt in the late sixteenth century, the eternal flame was rekindled by a spark from the lamp in Yamagata's Risshaku-ji (which had been lit with fire from Saichō's original flame). Thus, the flame has survived intact over the centuries and nothing—neither man-made or natural disasters, nor external or internal enemies, nor proponents of radical change or forces of extreme reaction—has been able to extinguish it. The flame has been

The eternal flame of the Dharma, kindled by Saichō 1,200 years ago, housed in the Kompon Chū-dō. (Courtesy of Enryaku-ji)

fueled and nurtured by generation after generation of dedicated Tendai practitioners with a "mind set on the Way." Regarding such true disciples, Saichō wrote: "One with a mind set on the Way is called a Bodhisattva in the West and a person of culture in the East. To take evil upon oneself and to give good to others, and to forget about oneself and to work for the benefit of all, is the ultimate in compassion."[3]

The two pillars of Tendai Buddhism are study and practice. The educational system on Hiei instituted by Saichō was the most thorough in Japanese Buddhism. The basic course lasted twelve years, divided into two six-year terms. As Saichō once declared, "Even the dullest stone becomes sharp after twelve years of daily polishing."[4] The first six years were devoted to theoretical "book learning." Two-thirds of the day was spent in general Buddhist and Tendai studies and the remaining one-third in liberal arts: Chinese classics, ancient science, literature, and the like. The second term was for practical implementation of knowledge obtained in the first: meditation, performance of rites, and engaging in one or more of the Tendai practices.

After the twelve years of retreat, Saichō wrote, "a Tendai priest should then be mature enough to work for the world: repairing reservoirs and irrigation ditches, reclaiming uncultivated land, restoring levees, constructing bridges and boats, planting trees, sowing fields, digging wells, and drawing water."[5] Tendai priests should know how to do more than just read sutras and cultivate their minds![6]

In the Kamakura period, the basic course was lengthened to twenty-one years: seven years of fundamental study under a master scholar-monk, seven years of Tendai doctrine, and seven years of contemplation.

Advanced Tendai education was quite similar to the system used in Tibetan Buddhism; that is, it revolved around public examinations and rigorous debate. There is a Tendai saying that "Buddha is more pleased when you debate the meaning of his sutras than when you merely venerate his words." Each temple maintained its own college for either exoteric or esoteric studies (depending on the course) with an endless series of debates and examinations for the candidates. Larger colloquia were held regularly in each of the major precincts of Hiei, and there were one or two mountain-wide debates each year in which scholars of forty years' standing matched wits with each other and the elder Tendai doctors. There was, finally, a Grand Debate conducted once every five years in the Great Lecture Hall. This debate is still held today, and successful participation in the meeting is mandatory for anyone who aspires to become *zasu* of Hiei. Today, Hiei Higher Academy carries on the tradition of Tendai scholarship.

Scholarship alone, however, will never lead to complete realization, for no philosophy, no matter how subtle or profound, can adequately encompass the whole truth—that must be experienced and realized through actual practice. As stated in the first chapter of the *Lotus Sūtra,* "Disciples of the Buddha cultivate all manner of practices, seeking the Path of Buddhahood."

The original Tendai practices were outlined by Chih-i, who was well aware that Tendai metaphysics had to be balanced with firsthand experience, that is, *samādhi* (Jap. *sammai*), identification with and grasping of a principle. The Chinese Patriarch recommended four types of *samādhi* (*shishū sammai*):[7]

1. Continuous seated meditation (*jōza sammai*). This involves ninety days of *zazen* (sitting meditation) with a determined effort to achieve total absorption in reality just-as-it-is. The practitioner sits in a bare hall, calming the mind and discerning the real, abandoning all limiting thoughts, in the hope that everything will unfold in crystal clarity. This practice, like all Tendai activities, is based on a verse from the *Lotus Sūtra:* "Abide in seclusion, cultivate the mind, and control the body, being as immovable as Mount Sumeru. Contemplate all elements as if they were not, as empty as space, void, neither produced nor existing, quiet and settled, fixed on the One."[8]

On Hiei, this demanding practice was apparently suspended in the nineteenth century but has been revived during the current Tendai renaissance. In 1964, the monk Horizawa Shōmon—who entered Hiei after abandoning his studies at Kyoto University—successfully completed the ninety-day term, and there have been several others since then. Trainees are secluded in one of the halls on Hiei—traditionally it was performed at Monjū-rō, but now Hokke-dō or one of the smaller temples are also utilized—and sit immobile in a meditation chair that provides some support for the head and back. Other than two toilet breaks and a few minutes of walking meditation each day, the practitioner sits in contemplation. Meals and a couple of hours of "twilight meditation" (i.e., sleep) are also taken in the lotus posture.

During the endless hours of *zazen,* Horizawa became immersed in his surroundings. He sang along (silently) with the birds and also heard the wind and rain "speaking" to him in incredibly beautiful tones. Other monks fared less well; rumor has it that at least one candidate went insane in the middle of the ninety days and ran screaming from the hall and down the mountain.

2. Continuous moving meditation (*jōgyō sammai*). This was the first Tendai practice on Hiei, instituted by Ennin, who learned the practice during his sojourn in China. For ninety days the practitioner circles a hall, endlessly reciting *"Namu Amida Butsu"* ("Hail to Amida Buddha!") while visualizing Amida's radiant form. The aim is to realize the Pure Land within one's own mind and, simultaneously, perceive the "emptiness" of conditioned existence.

On Hiei, this practice is carried out at the Jōgyō-dō Hall. The monk is allowed to sit down for his meals and given two hours a day to meditate-sleep in a chair. There are toilet breaks and a brief interval every twenty-four hours for the monk to leave the hall and rearrange his robes. At all other times the practitioner circles the hall over and over, chanting the *nembutsu* (See page 124 for Sakai Yūsai's experience of this practice.)

During the Middle Ages, this continual recitation of the *nembutsu* was very popular among Kyoto aristocrats, who flocked to the mountain in mid-August to attend a special three-day session.[9] Out of the practice evolved the Pure Land sects, which now dominate, numerically, Japanese Buddhism.

3. Half-moving, half-sitting meditation (*hangyō hanza sammai*). Although Chih-i described a number of different forms this practice may take, on Hiei it consists of a twenty-eight-day term (one week of preparation and three weeks of practice) at Hokke-dō, the hall ajoining Jōgyō-do. The practice involves performance of a Rite of Repentance six times a day—2:00 A.M., 6:00 A.M., 10:00 A.M., 2:00 P.M., 6:00 P.M., and 10:00 P.M. The rest of each day is spent chanting the *Lotus Sūtra* while circumambulating the hall, alternated with meditation on its contents while sitting.

4. Neither moving nor sitting meditation (*higyō hiza sammai*). This is free-style meditation in which all aspects of daily life are religious acts. It is the ability to be fully aware in whatever situation one finds oneself—the goal of Buddhist meditation. This is the most difficult of all practices, only for those well along the path of Buddhist training. In fact, Chih-i suggested that a good preparation for this ultimate meditation was latrine duty for eight hundred consecutive days, something that demands true presence of mind!

In addition to these classic Tendai practices, Hiei offers other forms of training. All candidates for the Tendai priesthood (both male and female) are required to participate in a sixty-day training period at Gyō-in, the Priest's Training Hall. The first thirty days are devoted to theory (*gegyō jishū*)—that is, sutra study, chanting practice, memorization of ceremonies, and then the Three Thousand Buddhas Rite, in which recitation of each of the names of the Three Thousand Buddhas (of the past, present, and future) are accompanied by a full prostration. The second month is centered on practical training (*shidō kegyō jishū*), consisting of actual performance of the rites and fire ceremonies during the night, daily purification in a waterfall, and, on the last day of the session, participation in *kaihōgyō*, the mountain pilgrimage of Hiei.

A priest who intends to remain on Hiei as an abbot of one of the numerous subtemples must then undertake a three-year retreat (*rōzan*). During the retreat, candidates select either the "Meditation Course" or the "Esoteric Rites Course" and

Immaculate Jōdō-in, site of Saichō's tomb and home of the "Cleaning Hell" and twelve-year mountain retreat.

are expected to perform at least one of the four traditional Tendai practices and experience one of the so-called "Hells" of Hiei:

1. The Cleaning Hell at Jōdō-in: a minimum of six hours a day cleaning the halls and grounds.
2. The Chanting Hell at Yokawa: total isolation indoors chanting and meditating.
3. The Walking Hell of Mūdō-ji Valley: the Hiei marathon of 100 days.

The ultimate Tendai training is the twelve-year retreat recommended by Saichō. These days, the retreat is performed at either Jodō-in or, in the case of *kaihōgyō,* at Mudō-ji Valley or Imuro Valley.

Among Hiei priests, the twelve-year retreat at Jōdō-in is considered the "test of tests." Jōdō-in is the site of Saichō's tomb and the Tendai Patriarch—like his counterpart Kūkai on Kōya—is thought of not as being dead but rather as in eternal meditation. Even though Saichō's physical form is not visible, his presence is keenly felt.

Thus, as soon as it is light enough for the retreatant to see his hand, he is up to prepare a meal for the Patriarch. After greeting the Master and serving him the food, the monk opens the temple doors to let the Tendai Founder assess the current situation on Hiei. The monk spends the rest of the day, each and every day for twelve years, attending the Patriarch, serving meals, chanting the *Lotus Sūtra* before him, and, above all, keeping the place spotless. Jōdō-in, "Hall of the Pure Land," is scrupulously cleaned and cleaned; the buildings must remain untainted by dust and grime and the garden free of leaves and weeds, the monk taking special care not to injure the tiniest insect in the process. All intercourse with the world is cut off; one robe and the thinnest bedcover suffice for the monk, summer and winter, in the heatless hall, and he subsists on leftovers—watery soup and plain rice—and three hours of sleep a day. After making his final report to Saichō at the end of the day, the monk closes the temple doors and retires to his room to study and meditate until midnight.

Not surprisingly, a candidate for the twelve-year retreat at Jōdō-in is very carefully selected. To ensure that they have the proper sanctity and resolve, the candidates must first survive *kōsōgyō,* the Practice of Visualizing Buddha. Day and night, the monk recites the names of the three thousand Buddhas, offering incense, ringing a bell, and then making a full prostration for each name. (In some cases, the monk also recites the complete monastic rules twice a day.) The monk is allowed only the briefest of rests for food and sleep (sitting up). He must continue until he "sees the Buddhas"; senior monks watch over him until they are satisfied that the vision is authentic. By the eightieth or ninetieth day, the monk is out of his mind with confusion and pain, unsure if he is alive or dead; suddenly, it is said, at the breaking point the monk experiences an extraordinary vision of peace and light. The monks are hesitant about revealing what they saw, but they are so transformed that they exist in a radiant, trancelike state for several months thereafter, virtually walking on air, without a need for sleep.

The monk remains on edge during the twelve-year retreat at Jōdō-in, acquiring a remarkable penetrating gaze and the keenest of senses. Because Jōdō-in can only accommodate one monk at a time, recently it has become common for the monk to spend ten years at Jōdō-in and then finish up the remaining two years at Shaka-dō in order to make room for the new candidate. To be sure, the twelve-year retreat is a real challenge. Of the 115 candidates since 1699, over thirty have died midway through the retreat. Four hearty souls, believe it or not, have served past the full-term, lasting fourteen, eighteen, nineteen, and twenty years on the job respectively. Nakano Eiken, the most recent retreatant, was bedridden for a year but is now recovered, full of fond memories of the twelve-year practice.[10]

The other twelve-year retreat centers around *sennichi kaihōgyō,* the 1,000-day marathon. Jōdō-in, naturally, is a major stop on the marathon course; when the monks who are constantly on the move for twelve years pass the temple, they bow silently to the monks who constantly stay put.

MOUNT HIEI TODAY [1]

HIEI flourishes today. The mountain monastery marked its 1,200-year anniversary in 1987 with several major celebrations including the "Hiei Summit," a gathering of international religious leaders to worship together and make a joint plea for world peace. More students, tourists, and serious pilgrims than ever flock to the mountain, and many of the old buildings have been, or are in the process of being, restored.

Hiei has five main peaks: Ō-bie-dake at 848 meters (2,782 feet); Shime-ga-dake at 838 meters (2,749 feet); Mitsuishi-yama at 675 meters (2,215 feet); Shaka-ga-dake at 753 meters (2,470 feet); and Mitsui-yama at 794 meters (2,604 feet). Japan is a wet country with lots of rain, which makes things lush (albeit damp), and the humidity on Hiei is always high. Although the mountain is situated in temperate western Japan, a combination of high altitude, tall trees that block out sunlight, and frigid air masses from Siberia turn Hiei into the "frozen peak" in winter. One section of the mountain is known as the Slope of Instant Sobriety. The cold there is so sharp and penetrating that it has the effect of sobering up the most intoxicated person in a few seconds. Snow blankets the mountain well into April, and flowers on Hiei bloom two months later than in Kyoto.

Hiei is a natural wildlife preserve. Hunting is outlawed, of course, and the mountain is full of forest animals rarely seen in such heavily populated areas—deer, boar, squirrel, fox, rabbit, badger, raccoon, weasel, bear (in the most isolated sections), and the famous Hiei monkey. The mountain is a bird-watcher's paradise, with over 850 species in residence, and the forests abound with unusual butterflies and other insects. The wildflowers of Hiei—violets, lilies, roses, daisies, and others—are another attraction.

Hiei is divided into three precincts. The Eastern Precinct (Tōtō) is the oldest section, containing the heart of the Enryaku-ji complex: the aptly named Kompon Chū-dō, "Hall of the Fundamental Middle." The huge building, the third largest wooden structure in Japan (and perhaps the world), is located on the site of Saichō's original monastery, which was of far more modest proportions. The present hall, which took eight years to complete, dates from 1642; it was constructed of materials donated, on orders of the Shogun, by all the feudal lords of the day.

Inside are housed Saichō's hand-carved image of Yakushi Nyorai and, before it, three lanterns glowing with the "eternal light of the Dharma." Saichō's image is a "secret Buddha" normally kept behind closed doors save for a few minutes at midnight on New Year's Eve. To celebrate the 1,200-year anniversary of Hiei, however, the sacred statue was on public display for a month and a half in the spring of 1987.

Flanking the Kompon Chū-dō is Monjū-rō. The hall of this "Pavilion of Mañjuśrī" is on the second floor. Previously, the practice of ninety days of seated meditation was conducted here, but nowadays the constant crowds create too much noise and the training is carried out elsewhere. Japanese students never fail to stop at this temple on their school trips, hoping that some of the wisdom of Monjū Bosatsu, the "all-knowing Bodhisattva," will rub off on them. Next to Monjū-rō is the Daikoku-dō, another shrine said to contain an image carved by the Tendai First Patriarch.

On the other side of Kompon Chū-dō is Daikō-dō, "The Great Lecture Hall." This is a new building, completed in 1963 to replace the former hall, which burned down in 1956. The once-every-five-years Grand Tendai Debate is held here, as is the annual Seminar on Buddhist Culture. In keeping with the ecumenical temper of the times, images of the founders of other sects who first studied on Hiei—Ryōnin, Eisai, Hōnen, Shinran, Dōgen, Nichiren, Ippen—are on display here. Down the road from the Daikō-dō is Amida-dō. This "Hall of Amida Buddha" was reconstructed in 1931. *Nembutsu* services are constantly conducted here, and many Tendai parishioners enshrine their ancestors' mortuary tablets in Amida-dō to benefit from the constant round of prayers.

In addition to the Kompon Chu-dō, the two most important sites on Hiei are the Kaidan-in and Jōdō-in. Kaidan-in is the Ordination Hall where Tendai priests receive the Mahāyāna precepts. This is the facility that Saichō gave his life for; without it there would have been no Tendai. The present structure, built in 1604, is not particularly impressive; it is the ideals which it represents that are inspiring.

Jōdō-in is perhaps the most haunting spot on the entire mountain. The "Hall of the Pure Land" is built around Saichō's tomb. The stately building, said to be based on a design of a Chinese temple of Wu-t'ai, sits unostentatiously back from the road. There is a definite feeling of light and peace about the quiet temple, and it is not difficult to sense the living presence of the Tendai Founder.

To the north of the Kompon Chū-dō is a tiny little hall called the Hongan-dō. Legend has it that Saichō lived on this site during his initial years on Hiei, carving all of his Buddha-images here, and the peaceful setting likely captures the ambiance of Hiei in Saichō's time. To the south is Mudō-ji Valley, home of the marathon monks. The main temples there are Myō-ō-dō, Benten-dō, Hōjū-in, Daijō-in, and Gyōkushō-in. The newest building in the Eastern Precinct is the Hokke Sōji-in, just recently completed. It contains the 1,000 copies of the *Lotus Sūtra,* the 500,000 *shakyō* sheets of the *Heart Sūtra,* and the 10,000,000 lines of Amida Buddha's name written by Tendai supporters and then presented to the headquarters, together with a donation of money, to pay for the construction of the building.

The main temple in the Western Precinct (Saitō) is Shaka-dō, the Hall of Śākyamuni. This building was originally the central hall temple of the Onō-ji complex at the foot of Hiei; it survived the conflagaration of 1571 and was moved to its present site in 1595 or so. Built around 1300, it is thus the oldest building on the mountain. The Buddha-image here, too, is said to have been carved by Saichō; it is kept hidden.

Nearby are the twin training halls of Jōgyō-do and Hokke-dō, mentioned above. Jogyō-dō, as the name implies, is for the practice of the ceaseless *nembutsu;* linked to it by a corridor is the Hokke-dō, the Hall of Lotus Meditation. There were similar halls once in the other two precincts, but they were not rebuilt. These buildings in the Western Precinct date from around 1600. The interior of both halls are bare save for, respectively, a single image of Amida Butsu and Fugen Bosatsu.

Perhaps the most interesting facility in this precinct is Kōji-rin, the "Lay

Part of the marathon monks' course now runs along a nicely paved highway, but at 4:00 A.M. there is no traffic to disrupt the monk's pace. ▸

Believers' Academy." From March through November, for a nominal charge, any interested individual or group may stay at the academy for a few days and experience life on Hiei. The director is a high-ranking Tendai master—for years it was headed by Horizawa Sōmen, the amazing monk who underwent the ninety days of seated meditation and the twelve-year retreat at Jōdō-in—and the daily schedule includes two periods of *shikan* meditation, a short pilgrimage to holy places on the mountain, group exercises (often jogging), sutra-copying, temple cleaning, Dharma talks, and formal vegetarian meals.

The Yokawa Precinct is the largest in area, covering the back and base of the mountain. Yokawa Chū-dō, the biggest temple there, was first established by Ennin, the developer of Yokawa, but like all the other structures on Hiei it has been repeatedly destroyed by fire. The present brightly painted structure, put up in the 1950s, is made of reinforced concrete—sure to last longer but not nearly as pleasing to behold.

The Nyohō-tō in Yokawa is the site of an important Tendai practice that dates back to the founding of Hiei. Ennin established an elaborate sutra copying ritual over a thousand years ago, and the same rite is still conducted today in strict adherence to the original procedure. The sutra-copying ritual held in this recently restored building attracts participants from all over the country; at least one attendance in the Nyōhō Sutra-Copying Ceremony of Hiei is thought to be obligatory for anyone who aspires to be a teacher of Japanese calligraphy.

Also in Yokawa is the Mount Hiei Museum, built in the 1930s to protect Tendai Art treasures and make them more available to the public. The influence of Tendai Buddhism on the development of Japanese art is profound, but discussion of that fascinating subject must wait until another time.[2]

The Training Academy (Gyō-in) mentioned above is located in Yokawa. Like Buddhist clerics of all sects in present-day Japan, most Tendai priests marry and raise families. While the majority of trainees at Gyō-in are sons or daughters of Tendai temples hoping to qualify for the priesthood during the sixty-day term, a surprising number of candidates are drawn from the general public—college dropouts searching for life's meaning, retired military men, remorseful ex-businessmen, reformed drunks, a handful of women, and occasionally a foreigner (one of whom has denounced the training at Gyō-in as the "worst experience of my life").

Imuro Valley is at the far end of Yokawa. As will be discussed in Part Two, this area has been restored and revitalized by three remarkable monks of the modern era.

At the base of Hiei lies the charming temple-town of Sakamoto.³ Sakamoto serves as a retirement village for aged Hiei priests and houses the administrative headquarters of the Tendai Sect. Hiei High School, the Hiei Higher Academy, and the Hiei Library are all in Sakamoto, making it the academic center of Tendai. A temple, Shōgen-ji, is maintained on what is thought to be Saichō's birthplace, and the tombs of all the recent Tendai *zasu* are located in this village. Hie (or Hiyoshi) Grand Shrine, seat of the powerful Shintō deity who protects Hiei, is in Sakamoto and there are dozens of other shrines and temples clustered about, many possessing gardens that rival the famous ones in the Zen temples of Kyoto. On the other side of Hiei is the Hiei International Hotel, noted for the delicious "warrior-monk stew" it serves.

Hiei is doing well these days, and that is good for all of us, for as an old saying has it, "When Hiei flourishes, the world brightens."

PART TWO

THE MARATHON MONKS

The path of a marathon monk is never-ending.
—Tendai saying

MOUNTAIN PILGRIMAGE

Sō-ō and the History of the Hiei Marathon [1]

The mountain itself is a *maṇḍala*. Practice self-reflection intently amid the undefiled stones, trees, streams, and vegetation, losing yourself in the great body of the Supreme Buddha.

—Attributed to Sō-ō

THE FASCINATING STORY of the marathon monks, perhaps history's greatest athletes, begins with the birth of the Grand Patriarch Sō-ō in 831. From an early age the boy refused to eat meat or fish and displayed scant interest in the toys and baubles that attract other children. At age fifteen he ascended Hiei and two years later received preliminary ordination. The young postulant lived simply in a tiny hut until he caught the attention of the abbot Ennin. Over the years, Ennin had noticed a young monk visiting the main temple every day, rain or shine, summer and winter, to offer incense and wild mountain flowers before Saichō's image of Yakushi Nyorai. Impressed by the monk's sincerity, the abbot offered to sponsor him as one of the Tendai sect's official government ordinands, but the monk suggested another trainee who spent hours and hours doing prostrations in the main hall.

Two years later an aristocratic candidate for the position of government ordinand decided to remain a layman and consequently asked Ennin to choose someone worthy to serve in his stead. The abbot selected the young pilgrim monk, giving him the name Sō-ō, "one who serves for others."

Ennin initiated Sō-ō into the Tantric mysteries of Tendai and also described the great mountain pilgrimages of Chinese Buddhism. Sō-ō was told about the Chinese monk "Priest Big Shoes," whom Ennin encountered there. This pilgrim monk circled the holy sites on the five terraces of Wu-t'ai for three consecutive years, completing fifty cycles in all. Amoghavajra, the master of esoteric science, had engaged in a similar practice when he first arrived in China, and a text composed in India clearly states: "Mountain pilgrimage on sacred peaks is the best of practices." [2]

Later in a dream, Sō-ō heard a voice telling him: "All the peaks on this mountain are sacred. Make pilgrimages to its holy places following the instructions of the mountain gods. Train hard like this each and every day. This is the practice of Never-Despise-Bodhisattva. Your sole practice is to be the veneration of all things; through it you will realize the True Dharma." Never-Despise-Bodhisattva, whose story is related in Chapter 20 of the *Lotus Sūtra*, did not recite sutras or read texts; his exclusive practice was to venerate all animate and inanimate beings, assuring one and all of future Buddhahood, even those who beat and abused him. This type of practice entails veneration of each blade of grass, each stone, seeing all things as a manifestation of Buddha, and worshiping nature with one's entire body and mind.

Following his formal ordination in 856, the twenty-five-year-old priest built a hermitage in what became known as Mudō-ji Valley. In 859, Sō-ō hid himself in remote Katsuragawa Valley in the Hira mountain range for a thousand days of austerities. Vouchsafed a vision of Fugen Bosatsu (Samantabhadra) one night, Sō-ō was thereafter blessed with immediate intuitive understanding of the sutras. Later, after a period of particularly intense meditation, Fudō Myō-ō appeared before Sō-ō in the Katsuragawa waterfall. Overcome, Sō-ō leaped into the falls to embrace the deity. Instead he collided with a large log, which he then dragged out and carved into the image of Fudō he had just seen. The image was enshrined, and the temple built around it was named Myō-ō-in.

The visionary monk acquired a reputation as a master of esoteric science and was considered to be a wizard. Over the years he was repeatedly summoned to the court to effect his miracles; Sō-ō's prayers cured terminal illnesses, difficult childbirth, demon possession, and imperial toothaches. Asked by the emperor what he wanted in the way of a reward, Sō-ō replied, "Declare Saichō and Ennin Great Teachers of the Dharma." The emperor did so in 865, proclaiming Saichō as "Dengyō Daishi" (Great Teacher Who Transmitted the Dharma) and Ennin as "Jikaku Daishi" (Great Teacher of Compassion and Enlightenment).

Upon completing his retreat in Katsuragawa, Sō-ō returned to Hiei and constructed a hall to house another image of Fudō Myō-ō. This hall, called Myō-ō-dō, became the home base of Hiei *kaihōgyō* monks. Sō-ō also established the Veneration of the Names of the Three Thousand Buddhas Practice. From December 31 to January 3 the names of the three thousand Buddhas are copied individually, accompanied by prostrations and chants.

In the tenth month of 918, Sō-ō sequestered himself in Myō-ō-dō, offered incense and flowers to the image of Fudō Myō-ō, sat facing the west, and serenely repeated the name of Amida Buddha as he entered eternal meditation. Upon his passing, it is said, the entire mountain peak was flooded with celestial music. Sō-ō is venerated as the father of Tendai Shūgendō, "the mountain religion of practice and enlightened experience."

Sō-ō's successor, Hengō, further developed Myō-ō-dō and Katsuragawa as centers of *kaihōgyō*. Hengō is traditionally believed to have done *kaihōgyō* for 3,600 days, representing ten years of continuous pilgrimage.

It is not clear exactly how *kaihōgyō* developed over the centuries because all the records on Hiei were destroyed in the pillage of the mountain in 1571. In its earliest form during the initial period 830–1130, *kaihōgyō* seems to have consisted of pilgrimages to places on Mount Hira and Mount Kimpu as well as on Hiei. It was largely free-style, depending on the predilections of the pilgrims.

With the establishment of all the main buildings and shrines on Hiei in the period 1130–1310, *kaihōgyō* to the Three Precincts of the mountain was formulated. It became a common practice for both Tendai priests and lay believers to make pilgrimages to the main holy places on Hiei. During this period, terms of 100 days, 700 days, and 1,000 days came into vogue.

Kaihōgyō as it is known today was largely developed in the third stage, from 1310 until the destruction of Hiei by Nobunaga in 1571. The manner of dress, the basic routes, and other procedures were codified in this period. A work called *The Story of Wandering Saints,* composed in 1387, describes the *kaihōgyō* of that era as consisting of a 40-kilometer (25-mile) course. The full term was 700 days with two nine-day retreats each year at Katsuragawa Valley. Upon completion of the

700th day, there was a nine-day fast at Myō-ō-dō, the same as today.

Kaihōgyō monks were the first to resettle on Hiei—after all, the only thing they needed for practice was their two feet—with the monk Kōun completing a 1,000-day term in 1583. Formal permission to rebuild Hiei was granted in 1585, and since then *kaihōgyō* monks have served as the mainstay core masters of Tendai Buddhism. There were three *kaihōgyō* routes: (1) Mudō-ji Valley Course (Gyokusen-ryū); Western Precinct Course (Shōgyōbō-ryū); and (3) Imuro Valley Course (Ekō-ryū). Five monks completed the 1,000-day *kaihōgyō* on the Western Precinct Course prior to its abandonment in the 1600s. The Imuro Valley Course, abandoned in 1590, has recently been restored by the priests Hakozaki and Sakai.

A twenty-year-old novice dressed up in the uniform of a marathon monk. Since he is only in his first 100-day term, he has not earned the honor of being permitted to wear the *gyōja* hat.

THE PATH OF
THE SPIRITUAL
ATHLETE

A *gyōja* (Skt. *ācārin*) is a spiritual athlete who practices (*gyō*) with a mind set
on the Path of Buddha. In Tendai Buddhism there is an appropriate practice
for everyone: "Those who cannot be saved through insight meditation should
take up the esoteric teachings; those who cannot be saved by the esoteric teachings should undergo some sort of religious practice." Of all the disciplines practiced
on Hiei, the mountain marathon—*kaihōgyō*—has had the greatest appeal over the
centuries, for it encompasses the entire spectrum of Tendai Buddhism—meditation, esotericism, precepts, devotion, nature worship, and work for the salvation of
sentient beings.

In principle, all Tendai priests and nuns must do *kaihōgyō* at least one day
during their training at Gyō-in. Men who wish to become abbots of one of the
subtemples on Hiei frequently opt for a 100-day term of *kaihōgyō*. The requirements
for the 100-day term are: to be a Tendai ordinand in good standing, sponsorship by a
senior Tendai cleric, and permission of the Council of Elder Gyōja.

If permission is granted, there is one week of preparatory training (*maegyō*)
before the term begins. The candidate is given a secret handbook (*tebumi*) to copy
which gives directions for the course, describes the stations to visit, lists the proper
prayers and chants, and contains other essential information. Because this handwritten manual is often damaged by rain and constant handling, the *gyōja* makes two
copies.

Also during this week, all the marathon monks of that particular term clear the route of debris, especially glass, sharp rocks, sticks, and branches, and piles of leaves in which vipers like to hide. While the new *gyōja* are rather lax about such clearing of the path, the senior marathon monks—who know what it is like to have their feet slashed or punctured by pointed objects or to step on a poisonous snake— cover every inch of ground thoroughly.

On day one, the *gyōja* suits up in the unique Hiei uniform and visits Sō-ō's tomb to ask for spiritual guidance. The pure-white outfit—made of white cotton only, for animal hair, skin, and silk are prohibited—consists of a short kimono undershirt, *nobakama* pants, hand and leg covers, a long outer robe, and priest's surplice. Around the waist goes the "cord of death" (*shide no himo*), with a sheathed knife (*goma no ken*) tucked inside; these two accessories remind the *gyōja* of his duty to take his life—by either hanging or self-disembowelment—if he fails to complete any part of the practice.[1] This is the reason the *gyōga* is dressed in white—the color of death—rather than basic Buddhist black. A small bag to hold the handbook, a sutra book, two candles, and matches is hung over the right shoulder; on occasion a flower bag to hold *shikimi* branches or food (offered at spots along the way) is draped over the left shoulder.[2] The *gyōja* carries his rosary in his left hand.

Inside the *higasa*, the distinctive woven "trademark" hat of the Hiei *gyōja*, a small coin is placed; if the monk dies on pilgrimage he will need the money to pay the boatman on the Oriental equivalent of the river Styx. Except for rain, the Great Kyoto Marathon (*kirimawari*), and the Katsuragawa Retreat, the *higasa* must be carried, not worn, by all *gyōja* with fewer than 300 days of training; it is always held in the left hand, and if put down it must be placed on the *hisen*, a special type of fan. The *higasa* is covered with the oiled paper when it rains. Since Buddhist monks and other religious pilgrims customarily wear large round straw hats, the reason for the peculiar elongated shape of the Hiei *gyōja* hat is uncertain, especially because it appears to afford less protection against sun, rain, and wind. On the other hand, one marathon monk believes that the length of the hat keeps branches away from the *gyōja*'s face and provides a clear view, two important considerations for those who walk along pitch-black mountain paths. The shape of the hat is also said to represent a lotus leaf breaking the surface of the water, signifying the emergence of Buddhist enlightenment in the midst of the world of illusion.

Eighty pairs of straw sandals are allotted for the 100-day term in Mudō-ji. For the longer Imuro Valley Course, *gyōja* are allowed the use of one pair per day. During the Great Marathon, the monk can use as many straw sandals as necessary, usually going through five pairs a day. This style of straw sandal is, like the hat, lotus-shaped and is thought to have originated in India. Most *gyōja* have their sandals made by a pious old grandma who lives in Sakamoto—her sandals are treasured as being both comfortable and good luck. In sunny, dry weather, one pair can last three or even four days, but in heavy rains the sandals disintegrate in a few hours. Thus the *gyōja* carries one or two spares.

The old-fashioned straw raincoat and the paper lantern, the other two permitted articles, are on occasion replaced in stormy weather by their modern counterparts—a vinyl raincoat and an electric flashlight. Rain—and in early spring, snow—is the bane of the marathon monks. It destroys their sandals, extinguishes their lanterns, slows their pace, washes away their paths, and soaks them to the bone. In years when the rainy season is especially bad, a marathon monk's robe never dries out completely.

The basic rules of *kaihōgyō* are as follows:

During the run the robe and hat may not be removed.

No deviation from the appointed course.

No stopping for rest or refreshment.

All required services, prayers, and chants must be correctly performed.

No smoking or drinking.

On the first day of the term, which begins at the end of March or the beginning of April, the new *gyōja* is accompanied by his master, who takes him through the entire course, giving his disciple various instructions and pointers. Thereafter the marathon monk is on his own. Since the *gyōja* is supposed to train alone, when there is more than one candidate (as has been the case every year recently), both the initial day of the run and daily starting times are staggered.

The day begins at midnight. After conducting (or attending) an hour-long service in the Buddha Hall, the *gyōja* munches on one or two rice balls or drinks a bowl of miso soup and then dresses. At Mudō-ji, the 30-kilometer (18.8-mile) journey commences at around 1:30 A.M. From Mudō-ji the marathon monk proceeds to Kompon Chū-dō and from there through the rest of the Eastern Precinct, then on to the Western Precinct, Yokawa, down to Sakamoto and back to Mudō-ji, stopping at 255 stations of worship and negotiating thousands of stairs and several

Marathon monks carry a handbook describing the course and the rituals that they must perform at each station of worship. The most important directions, however, are secret, given orally by a master to his disciple. ▶

very steep slopes along the way. At Imuro Valley, the course is longer, 40-kilometers (25 miles), with a few more stations of worship, and runs from Sakamoto up to the Eastern Precinct, Western Precinct, Yokawa and then back down to Imuro.

The stations include stops at temples and shrines housing just about every Vedic, Buddhist, Taoist, and Shintō deity that exists in the pantheons of those creeds; at the tombs of the Tendai patriarchs and great saints; before outdoor stone Buddha images; at sacred peaks, hills, stones, forests, bamboo groves, cedar and pine trees, waterfalls, ponds, springs; even a stop at one or two places to placate the gremlins or hungry ghosts residing there. At each station the *gyōja* forms the appropriate *mudrā* (ritual hand gesture) and chants the necessary *mantra;* the stops range from a brief ten seconds to several minutes. During the entire course the monk sits down only once—on a stone bench beneath the sacred giant cedar at the Gyokutaisugi, to chant a two-minute prayer for the protection of the imperial family while facing the direction of Kyoto palace.

Depending on the weather and the pace, the *gyōja* returns to the starting point between 7:30 and 9:30 A.M. The course can be conquered in six hours or even five and a half, but that is likely to draw criticism from senior monks, who disapprove of youngsters racing through the pilgrimage, hastily rattling off the chants and prayers. Most *gyōja* take between six and a half and seven and a half hours to complete the circuit.

Following an hour-long service in the main hall, the monk goes to his quarters to bathe and then to prepare the midday meal. After a simple, high-calorie lunch of noodles, potatoes, tofu, miso soup, and rice or bread, there is an hour's rest and time to attend to chores. At 3:00 P.M. there is another temple service. The second and last meal is taken around 6:00. By 8:00 or 9:00 P.M. the *gyōja* should be sleeping.

This routine is repeated daily without fail, one hundred times, with the exception of *kirimawari,* the 54-kilometer (33-mile) run through Kyoto. It occurs between the 65th and 75th days of the term, depending on the *gyōja's* starting date. In *kirimawari,* a senior marathon monk accompanies the new *gyōja* as they visit the holy sites of Kyoto and call on parishioners in the city. The new *gyōja* are thereby introduced to "practicing for the sake of others in the world." The freshmen receive more refreshment than usual during *kirimawari,* but they lose a day of sleep—

◄ Rain is the bane of runners everywhere. The marathon monk dons an old-fashioned raincoat in bad weather, though it does not offer much protection in a downpour.

kirimawari takes nearly twenty-four hours to complete, and almost as soon as they return to Hiei they must be out on the road again.

The freshman marathon monks have a very rough time. It takes two or three weeks to memorize the exact location of each station and the appropriate chants and *mudrās*. Before then, *gyōja* unfamiliar with the route sometimes get lost in the heavy fog that frequently blankets Hiei and go miles out of their way. Despite the cleaning of the pathways during the pre-training period, there are still plenty of sharp edges or points to cut tender feet to the quick. By the third day the legs and Achilles tendons begin to throb, and after a week they are painfully swollen. Cuts and sores become infected, and monks who were raised in the southern part of Japan often develop frostbite. Most monks run a slight fever the first few weeks, suffer from diarrhea and hemorrhoids, and experience terrible pains in their backs and hips. By the 30th day, however, the worst of the discomfort is over, and around the 70th day the *gyōja* has acquired the marathon monk stride: eyes focused about 100 feet ahead while moving along in a steady rhythm, keeping the head level, the shoulders relaxed, the back straight, and the nose and navel aligned. The monk also runs in time with the Fudō Myō-ō *mantra* he continually chants.

Following successful completion of a 100-day term and participation in the Katsuragawa Summer Retreat, a *gyōja* may petition the Hiei Headquarters to be allowed to undertake the 1,000-day challenge (*sennichi kaihōgyō*). This involves being free of family ties, willingness to observe a twelve-year retreat, and careful screening by the Council of Elder Gyōja. If accepted, the marathon monk follows the program as outlined in the table.

The first three hundred days are the basic training, the "boot camp" of the marathon monks. From the fourth year, the monks are allowed to wear *tabi*, Japanese-style socks, which considerably lessen the wear and tear on their feet. In the fourth and fifth year, though, the pace quickens to 200 consecutive days of running from the end of March to mid-October. Upon completion of the 500th day, the monk earns the title "White-Belted Ascetic" (Byakutai Gyōja) and may use a walking stick for the rest of the runs. He is also qualified to perform *kaji*, "merit

Top. During the entire run, the marathon monk sits down only once. There is a special stone bench beneath the mammoth sacred cedar at Gyokutai-sugi. The monk sits facing the imperial palace—and by extension all the people in the nation—to offer a prayer for peace and well-being. ▶
Bottom. During the Great Marathon, the monks stop to worship at all the major temples and shrines of Kyoto. ▶

[68]

transference" prayer services. Upon completion of the 700th day, the *gyōja* faces the greatest trial of all: *dōiri,* nine days without food, water, sleep, or rest.

A few weeks prior to *dōiri,* the monk sends out this invitation to the other Tendai priests: "I cannot express my joy at being allowed to attempt *dōiri.* This foolish monk vows to commit himself wholeheartedly to the nine-day fast, purify-

SENNICHI KAIHŌGYŌ
THE 1,000-DAY MOUNTAIN MARATHON OF HIEI

FIRST YEAR	100 days	30 (40) km each day one-day *kirimawari,* 54 km	*Shingyōja* (freshman). No *tabi;* hat carried
SECOND YEAR	100 days		No *tabi;* hat carried
THIRD YEAR	100 days		No *tabi;* hat carried
FOURTH YEAR	100 days 100 days	30 (40) km, *kirimawari*	*Tabi* permitted; hat worn from 301st day. Upon completion, *Byakutai Gyōja*
FIFTH YEAR	100 days 100 days		Wooden staff permitted from 501st day; on 700th day *dōiri,* 9 days without food, water, sleep, or rest. Upon completion, *Tōgyōman Ajari.*
SIXTH YEAR	100 days	60 km each day	*Sekizan Kugyō* (Sekisan Marathon)
SEVENTH YEAR	100 days	84 km each day	*Kyōto Ōmawari* (Great Marathon)
	100 days	30 (40) km, *kirimawari*	Upon completion (*mangyō*), *Daigyōman Ajari*
	1,000 days	38,632 (46,572) km	

Note: The numbers in parentheses are for the Imuro Valley course; all distances are approximate. From the second year, all monks participate in the Katsuragawa Summer Retreat, July 16–20. A secret rite known as the *Ichigassui* is usually performed once during the 100-day term.

◄ *Top.* The marathon monks pay their respects to the various Tendai patriarchs buried at different places all over the mountain. Here one of Sakai Yūsai's marathon dogs runs ahead of him on the path.

◄ *Bottom.* Although primitive in appearance, simple straw sandals such as these have served as "running shoes" for generation after generation of marathon monk.

ing body and mind, hoping to become one with the Great Holy One Fudō Myō-ō. Please join me for a farewell dinner." The *saijiki-gi,* the symbolic "last meal," is attended by all the senior priests on the mountain—a goodbye party to a *gyōja* who might not survive. This point is underscored by having the screens in the room reversed, just as they would be for a funeral.

Following the meal, a bell is struck at 1:00 P.M., and the senior marathon monks and other high-ranking Tendai prelates accompany the *gyōja* into Myō-ō-dō. The *gyōja* begins by making 330 full prostrations; after this, the guests depart, the doors are sealed, and the *gyōja* is left to his nine-day prayer fast.

At 3:00 A.M., 10:00 A.M., and 5:00 P.M. the *gyōja* chants the *Lotus Sūtra* before the altar. (During the course of the fast, the entire text is recited). At 2:00 A.M. he performs the *shusui* (water-taking) ritual. Chanting the *Heart Sūtra,* he walks to the Aka Well, about 200 meters from the temple, and scoops up a bucketful of water, carries it back to the main hall, and offers it to the image of Fudō Myō-ō. The remaining hours are spent sitting in the lotus position silently reciting the Fudō Myō-ō *mantra*—*"namaku samanda bazaranan sendan makaroshana sowataya untarata kanman"*[3]—100,000 times in all. It takes about 45 minutes to recite the mantra 1,000 times. Working in twenty-four-hour shifts, two monks, holding incense and candles, are always in attendance to make sure the *gyōja* remains awake and erect, touching his shoulders whenever he appears to be dozing off.

For several weeks prior to *dōiri,* the *gyōja* tapers down on his intake of food and water to prepare for the fast, usually limiting himself to one simple meal of noodles, potatoes and soup during this time. (He would usually not eat anything at the farewell dinner.) The first day is no problem, but there is some nausea the second and third day. By the fourth day the pangs of hunger usually cease. By day five, however, the *gyōja* is so dehydrated that the saliva in his mouth is dried up and he begins to taste blood. To prevent the sides of the mouth from adhering permanently, the *gyōja* is allowed, from the fifth day, to rinse his mouth with water, but every drop must be spat back into the cup. Unbelievably, the amount of liquid returned is often greater than the original amount. The drops that remain on the *gyōja*'s tongue

Top. During the Great Marathon and the Kyoto One-Day Run (*kirimawari*), the monks head up a colorful parade through the streets of Kyoto. Here Utsumi Shunsō leads the charge across Gyōja Bridge, one of Kyoto's landmarks. ▸
Bottom. The stations of worship encompass not only Buddhist holy sites. The Grand Shrine of Hie, seat of the important Shintō deity who guards Hiei, is a major stop on the run. ▸

are compared to the sweetest nectar. Defecation usually disappears from the third or fourth day, but very weak urination generally continues right to the end. Also from day five, the *gyōja* is given an arm rest when he recites the *Lotus Sūtra*.

The 2:00 A.M. water-taking ritual helps revive the *gyōja*. As he steps out of the hall made stuffy by incense smoke and poor circulation, the pure, bracing mountain air helps clear his head. *Gyōja* claim further that they absorb moisture from the rain and dew through their skin during this walk outdoors. The round trip to the well takes fifteen minutes the first day, but near the end it requires an hour, as the *gyōja* seems to move in a state of suspended animation.

The *dōiri*—the actual period without food, water, rest, or sleep is seven and a half days (182 hours)—is designed to bring the *gyōja* face-to-face with death. Hiei legend has it that the original period of *dōiri* was ten days; when almost all of the monks died it was shortened just a bit. It was further discovered that the humid months of summer were too dangerous—the deaths of the two *dōiri* monks mentioned in the modern chronicles both occurred in August—they rotted internally.

All the *gyōja* agree that the greatest ordeal of *dōiri* is not starvation or thirst but keeping the head erect and not being able to rest. It is interesting to note that the hardest part of making a Buddha image is the carving of the head. If the head is not perfectly balanced between the shoulders and on top of the body, sooner or later, it will fall off due to improper stress. Maintaining the correct posture at all times is the ultimate challenge.

During *dōiri*, the *gyōja* develop extraordinary sensitivity. They can hear ashes fall from the incense sticks and other normally inaudible sounds from all over the mountain. Not surprisingly, they can smell and identify food being prepared miles away, and they see beams of sun and moonlight that seep into the dark interior of the temple. At 3:00 A.M. on the ninth and concluding day, the *gyōja* makes his final trip to the Aka Well. A large crowd of upward of three hundred Tendai priests and lay believers gathers to attend the grand finale. The trip to the well, which only required twenty minutes the first few days of *dōiri,* now takes the weakened *gyōja* an hour to complete. He returns to the hall, sits before the altar, and bows his head as an official document from the Enryaku-ji Headquarters is read, proclaiming the end of the fast. The *gyōja* is then given *Hō-no-yū,* a special medicinal drink, to revive him. The final barrier is three circumambulations around the hall. When that is

◄ During their runs the marathon monks must stop at over 250 stations of worship. Here Utsumi chants a brief service before the Kompon Chū-dō.

done, the *gyōja* emerges from the "living death" as a radiant *Tōgyōman Ajari,* "Saintly Master of the Severe Practice."

Most *gyōja* report that they pass out for a second or two when they emerge from the temple out onto the veranda, in what is evidently a sudden transition from death back to life—for the *gyōja,* according to physiologists, who have examined them at the conclusion of the rite, manifest many of the symptoms of a "dead" person at the end of the *dōiri.* As *dōiri* nears conclusion, the *gyōja* experience a feeling of transparency. Nothing is retained; everything—good, bad, neutral—has come out of them, and existence is revealed in crystal clarity.

Some may condemn this type of severe training as a violation of Śākyamuni's Middle Way, but such death-defying exercises lie at the heart of Buddhist practice. There would be no doctrine of the Middle Way if Śākyamuni had not nearly fasted to death, subjecting himself to the most rigorous austerities to win enlightenment. Asceticism did not get him enlightenment, but it did lead to his transformation into a Buddha. This is why the emergence of a marathon monk from *dōiri* is compared to Śākyamuni Buddha's descent from the Himalayas following his Great Awakening. As one of the *gyōja's* relatives remarked, "I always dismissed Buddhism as superstitious nonsense until I saw my brother step out of Myō-ō-dō after *dōiri.* He was really a living Buddha."

Around 3:30 A.M. the *gyōja,* twenty to thirty pounds lighter, returns to his room, where he is greeted by his family and other well-wishers, receives a *shiatsu* massage, and sucks on chunks of ice made out of water taken from a miraculous spring on Mount Hira. The *gyōja* will then lie down for a few hours but only sleep about twenty or thirty minutes. It takes two weeks or so before he can take solid food; until then he lives on ice shavings, water, thin soup, *sake* or *amasake* (sweet, lightly fermented rice wine), and pudding. Nor does he sleep much the next several weeks, averaging two or three hours a night.

Following successful completion of the "seven hundred days of moving and the nine days of stillness," the *gyōja* are indeed men transformed. Grateful to be alive, full of energy, fortified by a vision of the Ultimate, constantly moving toward the light, and eager to work for the benefit of all, the monks head into the final stages of the marathon.

In the sixth year, the route lengthens to include a round trip to Sekisan-in at the base of Hiei (*Sekisan Kugyō*). The Sekisan Marathon along the extremely steep Kirara Slope—the slope used by Hiei warrior-monks of old to swoop down on

Kyoto—increases the course to 60 kilometers (37.5 miles), requiring fourteen to fifteen hours for stopping at all 260 stations of worship.

The seventh and final year again has two 100-day terms. The first—perhaps the supreme athletic challenge of all times—consists of a *daily* 84-kilometer (52.5 mile) run through the environs of Kyoto. The run encompasses the 30-kilometer walk around Hiei, the 10 kilometers of Kirara Slope, and the 44-kilometer circling of Kyoto. This is the equivalent of two Olympic marathons, and it is not run once every four years but performed 100 days in a row. During the aptly named Great Marathon (Ō-mawari), the monk sets out from Hiei at 12:30 A.M., covers the 84 kilometers over the next sixteen to eighteen hours, and then arrives, sometime between 4:00 and 6:00 in the afternoon, at a temple in the center of Kyoto to rest for a few hours. The following day, beginning at 1:00 A.M., the monk reverses the course. The course[4] was originally the city limits of Kyoto; the *gyōja* was thus circling the capital as he prayed for the protection of all its inhabitants, wise and foolish, saints and sinners, rich and poor, young and old alike. Nowadays part of the course cuts through the pleasure quarters of the city, past hostess bars, love hotels, strip joints, mah-jongg parlors, and pornographic theaters. The denizens of that world, too, receive the prayers of the marathon monk.

In addition to the three hundred or so stations of worship, the *gyōja* blesses hundreds of people each day (thousands on weekends and holidays). People of all ages sit bowing along the road to be blessed by the touch of the *gyōja's* rosary on their heads, diseased portions of their bodies, crippled limbs, hospital robes, or even on photographs of their loved ones. The *gyōja* is considered to be a vehicle, if not an incarnation, of the great saint Fudō Myō-ō, with the capability of transferring his merit to others. The Great Marathon is truly the practice of bestowing merit on others; while the monk's previous runs were solitary pursuits deep in the mountains, this marathon is for the benefit of all those struggling to survive in the midst of a big city, a silent turning of the Wheel of the Dharma, preaching by example rather than with empty words. Since the Great Marathon takes place in summer, the colorful procession of Tendai priests, lay believers, photographers and filmmakers, interested observers, joggers, and other assorted hangers-on literally stops traffic in the busy tourist season.

Negotiation of the 84-kilometer course is made somewhat easier by the use of a "pusher" on straightaways. A padded pole is placed at the small of the monk's back while the pusher applies a gentle force. If the pusher (a different person every day)

Top. Utsumi performing the *shūsui* (water-carrying) rite during *dōiri.*
Bottom. Sakai bowing with gratitude for being allowed to undertake the practice of *dōiri* and being able to complete it (*left*), and sipping a medicinal drink at the conclusion of the "living death" (*right*).

Two attendants guide Utsumi back to his quarters after *dōiri*.

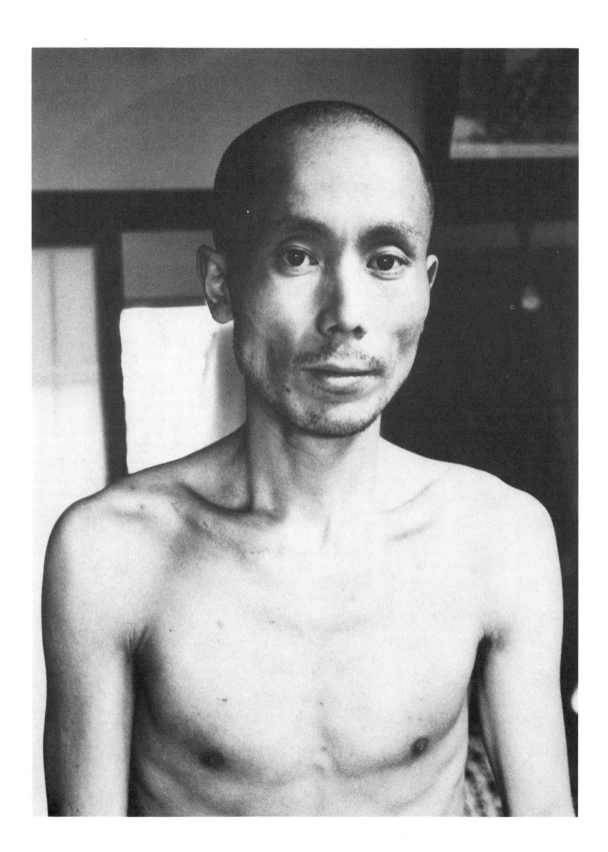

Left. Skeleton-thin but triumphant, Utsumi has just completed *dōiri;* notice his radiant eyes. *Above.* Two weeks later, he is fully restored.

The last great barrier the marathon monk faces on his quest is the 100,000-Prayer Fast. Day and night for eight days, the monk prays before the roaring fire lit before his patron, Fudō Myō-ō. The fire ceremony consumes all evil passions and purifies the consciousness.

has a lot of experience, he can supply as much as half the locomotion needed by the marathon monk on long stretches. If, on the other hand, the pusher is a novice or a young parishioner who cannot keep up with the monk, the extra assistance is nil. (Some marathon monks dispense with the pusher for part or all of the course.) Another attendant carries a small folding chair along, placing it down the instant the monk is held up by traffic lights or crowd control. Perhaps because of the constant encouragement and excitement of being welcomed by crowds of admirers, the *gyōja* come through the Great Marathon in surprisingly good shape despite the almost total lack of sleep. Such sleep as they do get is deep, sound, and refreshing. An old saying goes: "Ten minutes of sleep for a marathon monk is worth five hours of ordinary rest."

During the Great Marathon the monk is supported by dozens of *sokuhō-kō* parishioners. This special group of supporters accompanies the monk on his rounds, directing traffic and carrying equipment, preparing his meals, washing his clothes, and attending to his other needs. Some of the *sokuhō-kō*—the position is inherited from generation to generation—have been serving in this way for decades, covering nearly as much ground as the *gyōja* themselves.

The final 100-day term on the regular course is a snap; on day 1,000 the *gyōja*, who has run enough to have circled the globe, is declared to be a Daigyōman Ajari, "Saintly Master of the Highest Practice." Several weeks later the marathon monk vists the Kyoto Imperial Palace to conduct a special thanksgiving service known as *dosoku sandai*. When the emperor maintained his court in Kyoto, everyone had to remove his or her footwear before entering the grounds. A Hiei marathon monk was the sole exemption from this custom—he alone could enter the palace clad in straw sandals. The ceremony evidently originated with the *kaihōgyō* Patriarch Sō-ō's visits to the palace centuries ago to cure the imperial family's ailments.

There are two other practices integral to the 1,000-day marathon. The first is the annual Katsuragawa Retreat (Katsuragawa Geango) held from July 16 to 20. *Gyōja* who have completed at least one 100-day *kaihōgyō* term gather on Hiei on July 16. (Some *gyōja* from outlying districts walk hundreds of miles to get there.) Lining up in order of seniority (according to the number of retreats attended), the *gyōja* set out from Hiei at 4:00 A.M. for Mount Hira, 30 kilometers (18.8 miles) distant. The impressive body of *gyōja*—in certain years they can number as many as fifty—descend en masse from the mountain and pass through Otsu City on their way to Katsuragawa, arriving in the valley about twelve hours later.

During the retreat, the *gyōja* fast and conduct various rites. The highlights of the retreat are, first, the *taikomawashi* festival, in which the new *gyōja*, in imitation of Sō-ō's leap into the waterfall to embrace Fudō Myō-ō, bound off a large rotating drum and into a crowd of excited spectators; and, second, the secret rite at Katsuragawa in which the *gyōja*, firmly anchored by a lifeline, actually throw themselves into the cascading falls.

Since the Katsuragawa Retreat is devoted to the memory of Sō-ō, it takes precedence over all else, and marathon monks doing 200 days a year interrupt their running to attend. Thus the actual number of days on the road is more like 980 than an even 1,000, although recently the monks have been adding on the extra days after formal completion.

The final rite of the initiation for the marathon monks is the 100,000-prayer fast and fire ceremony, the *jumanmai daigoma*. One hundred days before the ceremony, the *gyōja* embarks on a stringent fast. All grains—rice, wheat, soy beans, and the like—plus salt and most leafy vegetables are prohibited. Consequently, the monk is obliged to live on potatoes and other root vegetables, boiled pine needles, nuts, and water. The fast dries the *gyōja* out, almost mummifying him, so that he will not expire of excessive perspiration during the eight-day fire ceremony in which he will sit in front of a roaring fire, casting in prayer stick after prayer stick. On each stick a supplicant has written a petition, which the *gyōja* "relays" to Fudō Myō-ō. Usually the number of prayer sticks exceeds 100,000, going as high in some cases as 150,000. Although this fast is one day shorter than that of *dōiri* and a few hours of sitting-up sleep is permitted, most *gyōja* feel that this is the greater trial—it is in the early stages, "like being roasted alive in hell."

Here again, the *gyōja* eventually becomes one with the fiery presence of Fudō Myō-ō, consuming all evil and purifying the world. The Great 100,000-Prayer Fire Ceremony takes place two or three years after completion of the 1,000-day marathon. It is not obligatory, but most of the modern marathon monks undergo it, partly to raise money for new construction projects—people donate money for each prayer stick that they write. Sakai Yūsai is the most recent monk to have done the ceremony, the sixth since the end of World War II.

Altogether there have been forty-six 1,000-day marathon monks since 1885. Two monks completed two full terms, one died (on purpose) on the 2,500th day of practice, and one, Okuno Genjun, did three full terms but without actually running each day during the third term. The majority of the marathon monks were in their vigorous thirties, while the oldest, Sakai, completed day 2,000 when he was sixty-one years old.[5] The number of monks who died or committed suicide on route is not known, but the path is lined with unmarked graves of *gyōja* who have been killed in action. No one has expired in recent memory during the 1,000-day marathon, but at least three monks perished in the nineteenth century.

How do the monks train for this ultimate marathon? Young novices build their strength by doing lots of manual labor—chopping wood, carrying heavy provisions from temple to temple, doing repair work on stone fences and stairs.

Food for practice: lunch during the Great Marathon. The meal includes fried noodles, miso soup with tofu and vegetables, sweet *yokan* jelly, and four kinds of liquid: potage, kudzu tea, an herbal tonic drink, and half a glass of milk. ▸

They also spend years acting as attendant to a senior marathon monk, accompanying the master while loaded down with baggage or acting as a pusher, matching the monk step for step.

What do they eat? The meals on Hiei are vegetarian—*shojin ryōri,* "food for practice"—and the monks thrive on what most modern athletes would consider a woefully inadequate diet. The following is a typical menu of a marathon monk:

1:30 A.M.	(before starting out): a bowl of miso soup with tofu
7:00 A.M.	(upon completion): miso soup, a bowl of rice gruel with daikon leaves, grated daikon with soy sauce
10:00 A.M.	herbal tea, honey and lemon water
12:00 NOON	(main meal): half a bowl of rice, noodles, boiled vegetables, tofu with sesame seed oil, *natto* (fermented soybeans), seaweed, pickles, and a glass of milk
2:30 P.M.	potato dumpling
6:00 P.M.	a bowl of rice gruel and soup

The marathon monks will occasionally take fish in the off-season and richer foods such as tempura, *yuba* (dried soybean cream), and sweets. Most favor several kinds of tonic drinks, concocted from herbs, lotus root, ginseng, and other secret ingredients. During the one hundred days prior to Jumanmai Daigoma, the monks subsist on buckwheat flour, nuts, potatoes, cabbage, and pine needles.

Older *gyōja* eat even less than the typical monk. Sakai, for example, takes two meals a day consisting of one plate of noodles, two boiled potatoes, half a cake of tofu with sesame seed oil, and boiled vegetables. This adds up to about 1,450 calories a day. According to modern dietary science, Sakai must use at least 2,000 calories during his 40-kilometer runs and therefore should be shedding ten to fifteen pounds a month. Far from wasting away, however, Sakai retains his robust physique, as seen in the photograph on page 88.

◄ *Top.* Joggers and young athletes enjoy accompanying the marathon monks on their rounds for the sake of their own training; no one, however, keeps up the pace for 100 days in a row.

◄ *Bottom.* Every year from July 16 to July 20, marathon monks past and present gather to participate in the Katsuragawa Summer Retreat. Here Sakai heads the procession from Hiei to Katsuragawa Valley.

▲ *This page.* After the monks arrive at Katsuragawa, they conduct various rites (*top*). The Drum-Turning Ceremony at Katsuragawa (*bottom*): In emulation of Sō-ō, founder of the Hiei marathon, new monks are required to leap onto a huge rotating drum and fly into the crowd. This re-creates Sō-ō's leap into the waterfall to embrace the image of Fudō Myō-ō.

◄ *Opposite page.* As soon as Sakai arises at midnight he performs *takigyō*, "waterfall training," to purify himself. Such purification is an important element in all Japanese religions, a method to cleanse both the body and the mind of impurities.

Dressed in rags (*left*), the monks also proceed to the actual waterfall (*above*) to reenact Sō-ō's leap.

Left. Fudō Myō-ō, the principle that the marathon monks come to embody. Fiercely devoted to the practice of Buddhism, Fudō will let nothing deter him from his appointed task of bringing all beings to salvation. His female counterpart is the beatific Kannon, the Goddess of Compassion. *Right.* Fudō Myō-ō represented by a mystic Siddhāṃ seed-syllable (*shūji*) drawn by the marathon monk Kanshūji Shinnin on the 900th day of *kaihōgyo*.

As mentioned above, marathon monks must get by on a minimum of sleep; consequently, they become expert cat-nappers, catching a few winks while waiting for traffic lights to change or at other lulls in their daily schedules. The monks learn to sleep sitting or even standing up, and most in fact prefer not to lie down to nap because that confuses their sense of time. Unsure of the correct hour, monks sometimes leap up from a mid-day nap, jump into their outfits, and race out of the temple. While on the road, they develop the faculty to rest different sections of the body as they move along—"Now I am resting my shoulders, now I am resting my hips, now I am resting my knees," and so on.

Other essential factors are proper rhythm, breath control, and intense concentration. The marathon monks harmonize their pace with the "beat" of the Fudō

Myō-ō *mantra,* which they chant continually, and cover meters and meters on each deep abdominal breath. An experienced marathon monk flows along naturally, maintaining the same speed for climbing up or coming down. The monks cannot allow themselves to be distracted by any obstacle, whether external or internal. They must be quite similar to the famed *lung-gom-pa* runners of old Tibet. Scores of explorers to Tibet and Mongolia recorded encounters with these running monks, who appeared to bound across the immense grassy plains; apparently in a trance, they could travel nonstop for forty-eight hours or more, covering over 200 miles a day. Since accomplished *lung-gom-pa* runners were faster than horses over long distances, they were often employed as a human "pony express" to convey messages across that huge country.

Interestingly, in order to qualify as a *lung-gom-pa* runner, a trainee first had to master seated meditation. Much emphasis was placed on breath control and visualization techniques—for example, imagining one's body to be as light as a feather. After acquiring good breath control, a novice was instructed to practice in the evening by fixing his gaze intently on a single star as he ran and coordinating his pace with a secret *mantra* given to him by his teacher. The runner must keep his eyes fixed on the star (or some other equally distant object) and never allow himself to be distracted. Once *lung-gom-pa* runners attained the proper level of moving meditation, they could fly like the wind, virtually gliding along in the air in a state of deepest contemplation.[6]

The marathon monks of Mount Hiei achieve similar results with their training methods, but the secret of their success lies in their spiritual rather than their physical strength. This spiritual strength—derived from the desire to realize Buddhahood, for the sake of oneself and the sake of others, in this very mind and body—is the key to the question "What makes the marathon monks run?"

Buddhism can never be understood purely through the intellect; it must be experienced: "Learn through the eyes, practice with the feet." The manner in which a suitable practice unfolds is known as *innen* in Japanese. *In* is composed of the inner factors, the stirring up of the Buddha-mind from deep within; *en* are the circumstances in which the drama is played out.

A man is drawn to Hiei and then to the path of a marathon monk. The *gyōja* have said that as soon as they don the robe of a marathon monk, all other concerns vanish; they gravitate toward the mountain paths, compelled by a powerful force that suffuses them with energy. The first 700 days of training are to enable the marathon monk to establish himself; it is a pilgrimage carried out in the immense silence of the Absolute on a remote, majestic, and mysterious mountain where gods and Buddhas dwell. Leaving behind the cacophony of the restless, relentless world, the monk isolates himself to live every day as if it were his last.

Midway on the marathon route the road narrows to a tiny footpath. To the left the runner looks down on Kyoto, a sea of lights wherein all the attractions, good and bad, that the world has to offer hold forth. To the right is Lake Biwa, sparkling in the moonlight, calm, clear, and empty. The marathon monk hovers briefly between the two spheres of worldly entanglement and Buddhist enlightenment and then presses on, hoping someday to transcend both.

In the last 300 days of the marathon, the focus shifts. The monk emerges from his hibernation, possessed of a certain measure of wisdom and compassion, to roam in a big city among all sorts of human beings, spreading light and happiness. A balance is struck between practice for one's own sake and practice for the benefit of all.

At the end, the marathon monk has become one with the mountain, flying along a path that is free of obstruction. The joy of practice has been discovered and all things are made new each day. The stars and sky, the stones, the plants, and the trees, have become the monk's trusted companions; he can predict the week's weather by the shape of the clouds, the direction of the wind, and the smell of the air; he knows the exact times each species of bird and insect begin to sing; and he takes special delight in that magic moment of the day when the moon sets and the sun rises, poised in the center of creation. Awakened to the Supreme, one marathon monk described his attitude thus: "Gratitude for the teaching of the enlightened ones, gratitude for the wonders of nature, gratitude for the charity of human beings, gratitude for the opportunity to practice—gratitude, not asceticism, is the principle of the 1,000-day *kaihōgyō*." Indeed, on the last day of the 1,000-day run, the monks have a saying: "The real practice begins from now."

The marathon monks are devotees of Fudō Myō-ō (Acala Vidyārāja), the Unshakable King of Light. Fudō has a fearful face, terribly troubled by the world's inequities, its stupor, and its implacable hatred of the Dharma. Encompassed by a fiery nimbus, Fudō burns up evil passions while illuminating the darkest corners of existence. His lasso can be used to bind devils or to pull those in distress out of the mud. Fudō's sword hacks off the heads of those who pollute the world but at the same time slices through all obstacles to reveal the deepest wisdom. As an incarnation of the cosmic Buddha Dainichi (Mahāvairocana), Fudō is the active element of salvation, capable of channeling his awesome power to others.[7] The marathon monks strive to become one with Fudō, to actually perceive that dynamic image as a living force and to tap that awesome energy. When questioned about this experience the marathon monks remain mum, but senior *gyōja* know when their disciples have had the vision, the greatest of all rewards: "You have seen him, haven't you? Now you have the look of a real marathon monk!"

RUNNING BUDDHAS

The Men Themselves

ALMOST nothing is known about the early *kaihōgyōja* of the modern era; the first reliable biographies date from the 1850s.[1] Gankai (1812–1873), *gyōja* number twenty-nine since the rebuilding of Enryaku-ji in the late sixteenth century, completed his 1,000-day term in 1853. That was the year Commodore Perry arrived on the scene, the first act in the drama that witnessed the fall of feudal Japan, the end of nearly three hundred years of isolation, and the emergence of the island nation onto the center stage of world history. Upon completion of his term, Gankai performed the traditional prayer service in the palace; the crown prince, later to become the emperor Meiji, was said to have been awed by the mysterious priest.

Gankai was a cosmopolitan Tendai monk who associated with most of the leading scholars, artists, poets, and imperial activists of Kyoto. After the Meiji Restoration in 1868, Gankai retired to Katsuragawa Valley, where he lived in a little hermitage guarded by two stone watchdogs—which, much to the monk's chagrin, were frequently mistaken for toads. Somewhat like the sixteenth-century eccentric Zen priest Fūgai, Gankai hoisted a flag outside his hut when he was short of supplies and then exchanged calligraphies and amulets for rice and other provisions. In

◄ Upon completion of the 700 days of movement and the nine days of stillness, a marathon monk is a man transformed. Hereafter his practice will be for the sake of others, and much of his time will be spent transferring his merit to the thousands of people who bow along the pilgrim path by blessing them with a touch of his rosary.

classic *yamabushi* ("mountain priest") style, Gankai ended his colorful career by throwing himself, in a state of rapture, into the waterfall at Katsuragawa.

Gōshun (1828–1902), *gyōja* number thirty, completed his 1,000-day term in 1860. Not much information is available about this monk; after completing *kai-hōgyō* he continued training quietly in and around Hiei for the rest of his days. Kakuhō (1807–1890), the next *sennichi kaihōgyōja,* completed his 1,000-day term in 1864 at the advanced age of fifty-seven. A respected scholar, Kakuhō restored the monastic library of Enryaku-ji and founded the first elementary and high schools on Hiei. This scholar-practitioner-educator became the 234th *zasu* of Tendai in 1879, the first (and so far the only) *kaihōgyōja* to have assumed that position. *Gyōja* number thirty-two, Kōjun (d. 1885), was another outstanding scholar-practitioner of Tendai. Kōjun was well known for his breadth of learning and his tenacity in debate—his nickname was Priest-and-Furthermore. In contrast to the vast majority of *kaihōgyōja,* who tend to be stocky, sturdy types, Kōjun was small and delicate—his success in the most demanding of all practices was a prime example of mind over matter. Kōjun was the last *gyōja* to perform the imperial prayer service in the actual presence of the emperor (in 1865). After the Meiji Restoration, the imperial court was moved to Tokyo.

Genshin (1850–1918), *gyōja* number thirty-three, completed his 1,000-day term in 1886. Not much of a scholar, Genshin was a big, burly fellow over six feet tall. His strength and endurance are legendary: unlike the other *gyōja,* Genshin did much of his walking in midwinter, withstanding freezing temperatures and heavy snow. The next successful *gyōja* was Kakunin (1867–1921), who finished in 1903. He was a former samurai who became a monk on Hiei after concluding a vendetta. Although not nearly as large as Genshin, Kakunin too had a reputation as a strong man.

Two years after Kakunin, Kanjun (1862–1913) finished his first 1,000-day term. Kanjun was originally a storekeeper in northern Japan. When in his mid-thirties, he stood by helplessly as a boatload of people drowned in a flooded river, and the shock caused him to abandon his home and business. On Hiei, Kanjun threw himself into training, spurning the opportunity to assume the abbacy of a temple. When he was not walking, he was performing full prostration after full prostration—the *tatami* mats in his little hut had deep holes where his forehead, elbows, and knees struck the floor. After completing an initial 1,000-day term at age forty-three, Kanjun continued on to a second term, finishing in 1910. Then, on the 2,500th day of pilgrimage, he came to his favorite place on the *gyōja* path, a lovely spot in Mudō-ji Valley overlooking Lake Biwa, neatly arranged his articles and his robes, sat down, and serenely passed away beneath a stone Buddha he especially liked. While the first 1,000-day term must be carried out in the established manner, quite a bit of leeway is allowed for those who are Daigyōman Ajari—after all, they are living Buddhas! Thus, Kanjun did the second half of his pilgrimage at a leisurely pace, pausing here and there to enjoy the view, having a snack from the box lunch he brought along, or chatting with passers-by. In common with the other *gyōja*, Kanjun was severe with himself but kind and considerate toward the many lay people who sought his counsel, with the exception of those who tried to impress him with their social standing—such "dignitaries" were sure to be kept waiting for hours and hours.

Gyōja number thirty-six, Genjun (1874–1941), was once a clothing merchant. In his early thirties he renounced the world and made his way to Hiei, where he kept a vow of silence for some years. Genjun completed his first 1,000-day term in 1918, at age forty-four; the second in 1926, at fifty-two; and the third in 1934, at sixty. However, Genjun went lame sometime during the third term and, in keeping with his privilege as a Daigyōman Ajari, he had porters carry him around the route in a palanquin; consequently his feat is not quite as impressive as it sounds. Genjun was short but muscular, and he is said to have virtually bounded through the mountains at a rapid clip. In addition to his athletic skills, Genjun was an accomplished master of the tea ceremony, flower arrangement, and geomancy. He was reputed to be a wonderworker as well, capable of curing people of illness, sometimes just by chanting a *mantra* over the telephone. The somewhat mysterious Genjun was the last of the old-fashioned *gyōja*.[2] The ten *gyōja* of the present Shōwa era (beginning 1926) are modern men in every sense.

One of the most colorful *gyōja* of this (or any other) era is Hakozaki Bunno,[3] who was born in 1892 to a poor family in Iwaki, a fishing village in northern Japan.

Pages 100–103. Along the crest of Hiei, the monks look down on serene Lake Biwa to the east and sparkling Kyoto to the west, poised between the two worlds of Buddhist emptiness and worldly attractions. ▶

Since there was not enough work in the tiny seaport, Hakozaki wandered about northern Japan and Hokkaidō, hiring himself out as a fisherman or dock hand. The rest of his time was spent drinking and brawling. Some say that Hakozaki had a change of heart one day after waking up in a jail cell following a drunken spree; others maintain that his conversion came about as a result of seeing some of his best friends drown in a boating accident. Another account has it that Hakozaki, a despondent vagrant, tried to hang himself in a park and was cut down just in the nick of time by a Tendai priest who directed him toward Hiei. Perhaps all three stories have some truth to them.

At age thirty-five, the day laborer entrusted his long-suffering wife and child to relatives and begged his way to Hiei. The priests there wanted nothing to do with this strange-looking man dressed in rags and with filthy, matted hair. One kindly monk, however, took pity on him, sending him along to the temple of the *kaihōgyōja* Okuno Genjun. At that time, the crippled Genjun was being carried around the route in a palanquin, and extra hands were always welcome. The powerful Hakozaki was taken on as a porter, but one day he and the other carrier took a turn too quickly and the old abbot went tumbling out of the palanquin and fell halfway down the mountain. The other, more experienced porter naturally blamed the mishap on Hakozaki, who was dismissed from the temple on the spot. Hakozaki drifted over to Daijō-ji, another large temple on Hiei, and sought admittance as a lay attendant. Having heard of his reputation, the abbot, Ōmori Buntai, absolutely refused. The desperate Hakozaki thereupon sat himself down in the temple garden and declared, "Either you let me in or I will die!" Hakozaki remained rooted there for four days without food or drink, not budging even after being splashed with buckets of ice-cold water and swatted with a broom. On the fifth day of his fast to the death, the abbot relented.

Thereafter the fiercely determined Hakozaki outshone all the other *gyōja* on Hiei. He was ordained in 1931, at the late age of thirty-nine, and performed *sennichi kaihōgyō* from 1934 to 1940 without the aid of a single assistant. Daijō-ji was an extremely busy temple, and Hakozaki slaved away at temple chores all the while he was doing *kaihōgyō*—frequently picking up equipment and provisions for his temple during his daily pilgrimages and carrying them back up the mountain. Hakozaki always marched to a different drummer. The headstrong monk made a number of changes in the route and established procedures based on his research on the oldest *kaihōgyō* texts. Several of the senior monks were upset by the upstart's actions and disputed Hakozaki's right to be called a Daigyōman Ajari; one particularly vociferous critic wanted him expelled from Hiei altogether. To avoid further controversy and gain deeper insight into *kaihōgyō,* Hakozaki temporarily left Hiei in 1942 to train in Omine, site of a different *kaihōgyō* course. Normally a *gyōja* would alternate between Omine and Yoshino, making a one-way trip of twenty-four kilometers (15 miles) each day. Hakozaki thought this not challenging enough and thus made round-trips each day for three weeks. When they saw Hakozaki zooming along the precipitous mountain paths, the locals wondered to themselves, "Who is that superman?" Hakozaki made extensive "inspection tours" in the area for another twenty-nine days and then embarked on an extensive 120-day pilgrimage to western Japan, training at other sacred mountains such as Ontake and Fuji, while subsisting mostly on air and water.

Hakozaki's critics on Hiei eventually passed from the scene, and the eccentric monk was assigned to Chōjū-in, a small temple in a remote section of Imuro Valley. Chōjū-in had been semi-abandoned for years before being restored by Hori Kakudō, another unusual monk whose career parallels that of Hakozaki.

A former soldier who served in the Seinan War against the diehard forces of Saigō Takamori, Kakudō could not fathom why some men perished in the fighting and why others, like him, survived. When he was reunited with his wife after his discharge, he was inconsolable: "I'm happy to see you, but what about the wives and children of the men I helped kill?" Overcome with the world's fragile impermanence, Kakudō left home to seek the answers to his questions.

Kakudō ended up on Hiei and Imuro Valley, where he put up a makeshift little hut. Every morning for the rest of his life, he rose at 2:00 A.M., chanted the *nembutsu* 10,000 times, and then spent the rest of the day clearing the land, working in the fields, restoring the Fudō-ō and Chōjū temples, digging wells and ponds, constructing roads, and making Tendai rosaries for the local folk.

When Hakozaki took over from Kakudō, he continued to farm and further improve the valley, his most notable accomplishment being the restoration of Imuro Valley *kaihōgyō* course after four hundred years of neglect.

Every year from 1948 to 1973, Hakozaki secluded himself in the Hira Mountains north of Hiei for a seven-week retreat. Hira is the source for much of the water that nourishes the Kyoto area, and the ex-fisherman had a special affinity for that precious resource—he prayed and fasted in hopes of keeping the springs there pure and uncontaminated. The tireless Hakozaki constructed roads there too and excavated several cave hermitages for religious training. Once during a cloudburst, a young mountain climber on Hira scrambled into one such cave and came face to face with Hakozaki, in the middle of a nine-day fast, sitting immobile in the lotus posture. Receiving the shock of his life, the young man leaped out of the cave and headed straight down toward the town, mumbling wildly about the wizard he had encountered.

Hakozaki has undergone the nine-day fast of no food, water, or rest an unbelievable thirty-six times—frequently at year's end to cleanse his body for the coming year and as an expression of gratitude for everything he received in the past twelve months. He has been blessed, reportedly, with spectacular visions of the Vajra Kings and other members of the Buddhist pantheon. Hakozaki's motto is: "If you are not afraid of death, you can achieve anything. Put your life on the line and great enlightenment will be yours!" He has also declared: "I practice because I am a Tendai priest. It is the natural thing for me to do. I walk and walk filled with gratitude, ever mindful of the kindness I have received from all quarters. If a priest does not train sincerely, he will be asking for a super-express ticket straight to hell."

Even though Hakozaki lost his eyesight and most of his ambulatory power in his eighties, he continued to rise each morning at two o'clock to purify himself in the two sacred waterfalls at Chōjū-in until just recently (he is ninety-five years old at this writing). He now passes his days serenely with the name of Amida Buddha constantly on his lips.

One of Hakozaki's more endearing traits is his love of rice wine (*sake*), the "hot water of transcendental wisdom." In his eighties, Hakozaki began drinking this best of all medicines again, to ease the pains of old age, and enjoyed nothing better than to toss a few down with convivial companions. He has told young monks that if they think of *gyō* as torture of the body or subjection of the flesh they will destroy the practice. "The purpose of *gyō*," the ancient sage says, "is to discover the joy of life."

Enami Sōken, the second *sennichi kaihōgyōja* of the Showa period and number thirty-eight in modern times, underwent the discipline in response to those on Hiei who wished to abolish the practice. "*Kaihōgyō* should be banned in this age of science," certain secularized priests declared. "The practice is riddled with superstition and is an outmoded relic of folk religion. Hiei should produce scholars of pure Buddhism, untainted by accretions and bizarre customs."

Enami, who was born in 1903, was intent on restoring Tendai Buddhism as a force in the contemporary world by repairing and rebuilding the temples on Hiei, reestablishing traditional training, and raising as many fine monks as possible. Even though he was extremely busy with the supervision of various construction projects, he realized that if Hiei ceased to be a center of training, all was lost. Enami therefore undertook the traditional *kaihōgyō* practice, doing most of his walking during the disastrous war years (he finished in 1946), convinced that the future of Tendai revolved around the two pillars of study and practice.

Enami Sō-ken trained over four hundred disciples, and virtually all of the top *gyōja* of the modern period were his students. A scholar, practitioner, and storyteller in the best Tendai tradition, he was immensely popular with lay people, whom he invariably greeted with a big smile, cup after cup of tea, and piles of fruit and sweets. Every visitor, though, was told to bring something—news of himself or herself and of the world at large. Everything Enami received he shared with others, and although he was very strict with his personal disciples, censuring their slightest infractions in a big booming voice, he was considered by one and all as the "Restorer of Hiei," and his passing in 1971, of pancreatic cancer, was a great loss.

The primary popularizer of *kaihōgyō* is Hagami Shōchō. Hagami was born into a Tendai temple family in Okuyama Prefecture in 1904. Hagami received preliminary ordination as an elementary school student (as is the case with most "temple children"), majored in German philosophy at the University of Tokyo, and then became an instructor at Taishō University, a Buddhist educational institute. A noted bon vivant and gourmet of western dishes, the young professor married a brilliant fellow student—the story of their love affair was fictionalized as a novel by one of their writer friends and later made into a movie—and was on his way to a promising career as an academic. The death of his pretty young wife at age thirty-one of tuberculosis brought the fairy tale to an end, however, and the despondent Hagami, then thirty-three years old, resigned his university position and returned to his impoverished home temple.

During the war years Hagami became a fanatical opponent of Japan's surrender and wrote a series of articles urging his country to fight to the last man, woman, and child. Even after the emperor's broadcast announcing the end of the war, Hagami refused to believe that Japan had been defeated. Through his contacts with the newspapers, he obtained a press pass enabling him to attend the surrender ceremony on the *U.S.S. Missouri.* Hagami managed to position himself on the ship's bridge, and if General MacArthur or any other of the American delegation slighted the Japanese contingent in any way, the temporarily deranged reporter planned to throw himself off the bridge on top of MacArthur in one final *kamikaze* attack. The dignified general, of course, was a perfect gentleman, and Hagami came to his senses. In fact, after later learning that MacArthur had stated that all Japanese are emotionally twelve years old, Hagami decided to enter Hiei, train intently, and then devote himself to elevating the spiritual level of his fellow Japanese.

Hagami asked to be accepted as a disciple of Enami Sōken. When Enami saw Hagami for the first time, he said to the novice monk, "You look like an egghead in those thick glasses. Take them off!" Hagami was terribly nearsighted, but he followed the master's orders and quickly learned to negotiate his way around the mountain with the "eyes of the heart."

Even though Hagami was rather delicate as a youth and had not exercised much as a college professor, he was inspired by his master's example and undertook the arduous *sennichi kaihōgyō* as his main practice. In his third year of training, the *zasu* appointed him principal of the Hiei High School. When Hagami protested that he would never be able to administer a high school while engaged full-time in *kaihōgyō,* the chief abbot told him: "You do not have to say or do anything. All I want from you is to come to the high school in your *gyōja* robes, directly after you finish the daily course, chant a sutra with the students, and encourage them to 'Keep at it!' That is the best education they can receive."

In the aftermath of Japan's surrender there was a severe food shortage which was particularly bad on Hiei. Hagami and the other *gyōja* survived on wild vegetables, berries, pine needles, and bamboo shoots—he recalls dandelion greens as being especially tasty.

Hagami completed his 1,000-day term in 1953 and the 100,000-prayer, eight-day fast and fire ceremony the following year. Then he performed *unshin kaihōgyō,* a kind of mental mountain pilgrimage. In this variation, the practitioner rises every day at 3:30 A.M. for 1,000 consecutive days, sits on the veranda of Myō-ō-dō, and walks through the *kaihōgyō* course in his mind, reciting the appropriate chants and forming the required *mudrā*s. Then Hagami embarked on still another 1,000-day term, this time of "half-moving, half-sitting" practice, for a combined total of 3,000 days of classical Tendai training. The rest of his life, Hagami hopes, will be spent in the ideal "practice beyond practice."

Hagami has written two books on *kaihōgyō* and other Tendai practices and lectures widely at home and abroad.[4] He is noted for wise counseling of professional baseball players, Japan's top athletes. (Members of teams in Tokyo generally seek out the advice of Zen masters, while those in western Japan typically consult with the Ajari of Hiei.) Hagami once gave this sage advice to a disgruntled player who complained, "Last year I won the home-run title, but this season the management cut my salary to help pay for the big bonus they offered a rookie pitcher. That is unfair, and I'm going to quit baseball!" Hagami advised, "Forget about venting your spleen on the system and the people who control it—that will produce nothing. Take out your anger and frustration on the baseball." The player followed Hagami's directions, captured the triple crown, and won a big pay hike.

Hagami once conducted a seven-day *kaihōgyō* training session for Japanese businessmen. Intriguingly, he discovered that the experiences of the businessmen for each progressive day paralleled the emotions felt by the marathon monks during the successive years of training:

FIRST DAY:	"Tough but interesting."
SECOND DAY:	"How did I get myself into this?"
THIRD DAY:	"I'm going to die."
FOURTH DAY:	"Hang on—maybe I can make it."
FIFTH DAY:	"Things are looking up."
SIXTH DAY:	"Only one more day left."
SEVENTH DAY:	"I did it! All in all, it wasn't so bad."

In a complete reversal, Hagami—a onetime ultra-right-wing nationalist, has become a prominent figure on the international scene of world disarmament and ecumenical understanding. In 1977 he visited the Egyptian president, Anwar Sadat, who at Hagami's urging agreed to sponsor a joint prayer service on Mount Sinai for world peace. Hagami has met with the Pope and many other prominent Christian, Jewish, and Muslim religious leaders. He holds a high position in the Tendai hierarchy and was one of the principal architects of the Hiei Summit of World Religions held in August 1987. The Tendai monk is also president of the Kyoto branch of UNESCO.

Perhaps because of these "political" activities, criticism of Hagami is occasionally voiced in regard to what Americans would call his "grandstanding." For a *gyōja*, Hagami seems to crave the limelight a bit too much, and despite his good intentions, he clearly enjoys associating with the religious and secular powers-that-be.

In contrast to the familiar figure of Hagami, the four *sennichi kaihōgyōja* who succeeded him tended to keep to themselves and are not well known at all. Kanshuji Shinnin, from an ancient aristocratic family, finished his term in 1954 at the advanced age of fifty-five. He died a few years ago. Enami Kakushō, adopted son of Sōken, completed his term in 1960; Kobayashi Eimo finished his term in 1961, and Miyamoto Ichijō his in 1962. All three now serve as abbots at Hiei subtemples.

The first *gyōja* to be prominently featured in the Japanese mass media was Mitsunaga Chōdo.[5] He was born to a farm family in Yamaguchi Prefecture in 1937. Mitsunaga's father was killed in an air raid during the war, and the orphan was adopted by an older sister and her husband, who happened to be a Tendai priest. Frail and moody as a youth, Mitsunaga was totally uninterested in Buddhism. After high school he worked as a blacksmith for a time, then spent several years as a hard-drinking drifter. Mending his ways, Mitsunaga reconverted to Tendai and became the disciple of Enami Sōken. In 1970 Mitsunaga completed his 1,000-day term, the 100,000-prayer, eight-day fast and fire ceremony in 1972, and his twelve-year mountain retreat in 1975.

Initially, Mitsunaga refused all requests for interviews and photographs, declaring "I'm not an actor!" However, when a newspaper reporter threatened to write that the *gyōja* on Hiei were selfishly pursuing enlightenment for their own sake and cared nothing about the suffering of humanity, Mitsunaga relented.

Although he appears to be a no-nonsense, straightforward individual, Mitsunaga's experience of *kaihōgyō* was perhaps the most "mystical" of all the modern *gyōja*. Apparitions frequently appeared to him on his nightly rounds, ranging from the ghastly (suicides with ropes around their necks or poison dripping from their mouths, pleading to be released from their suffering) to the heavenly (glorious visions of the Tendai saints). He learned the languages of the birds and beasts and during *dōiri* had an out-of-body experience, feeling himself soaring among the clouds with the birds that flocked around Myō-ō-dō.

Once he was asked by an announcer on a radio program, "What did you gain from *kaihōgyō?*"

"Nothing," Mitsunaga replied immediately. "Nothing at all. All I learned is that I was walking in the palm of Buddha's hand."

After finishing his twelve-year confinement, Mitsunaga did a great deal of traveling and took delight in rediscovering the joys of the world below. He has never adjusted to hotel rooms, though; the tiny concrete quarters seem like lifeless tombs, and his heart is never far from the majestic pines and deep valleys of Hiei.

The two most recent *gyōja,* Utsumi Shunshō and Sakai Yūsai, have attracted the greatest attention, becoming the two superstars of contemporary Japanese Buddhism.

The engaging Utsumi Shunshō, the subject of the majority of photographs in this book, was born in Shikoku in 1943.[6] His father, a prosperous clothing merchant who provided the uniforms for the Japanese Imperial Navy, was also active in the field of welfare for the blind, establishing a Braille library on his own estate and building a school for the sightless in the town. With Japan's defeat the factory lost most of its business, however, and when Utsumi was a sixth-grader, the factory was declared bankrupt and the family lost everything.

Long interested in religion and with many relatives who were Buddhist clerics, Utsumi's father decided to become a Tendai priest and opened a little temple. Both Utsumi and his sister were ordained, and he was sent to a larger temple in Zentsu-ji City for formal training. After completing junior high school in Shikoku, the promising young novice was sent to Hiei for advanced studies, receiving special entrance to Hiei High School on the strength of recommendations given by the top Tendai priests in Shikoku.

Utsumi was then assigned to serve as the attendant of Enami Kakushō, the young abbot of Gyokushō-in in Mudō-ji Valley. Kakushō was only thirty-one years old at the time, and Utsumi was his first disciple; since Kakushō was in the midst of *sennichi kaihōgyō,* Utsumi, the sole trainee, was busy from morning to night attending to temple chores and accompanying his master on the midnight pilgrimages. Despite those heavy burdens, Utsumi was required to have perfect attendance at Hiei High School and maintain high marks, which he did.

During his tenure as his master's "pusher," Utsumi developed great respect for Kakushō's stamina and devotion to training. To be a good pusher, one has to match one's stride and bearing with that of the *gyōja;* indeed, if he does not become one with the master, the pusher actually becomes a hindrance rather than a help. As a pusher, Utsumi built up the power of his legs, learned the proper stride and correct posture, and acquired a feel for the subtleties of *gyōja* practice.

Utsumi was given permission to do the 100-day marathon in 1966 when he was twenty-three years old. He wanted to attempt the full 1,000-day pilgrimage, but Kakushō felt that he needed more seasoning. Consequently, Utsumi spent the next eight years studying at the Hiei Higher Academy, working out with the Hiei High School baseball team, and making a trip to the Buddhist sites of India. In 1974 Enami gave Utsumi the go-ahead, and the thirty-one-year-old monk set out to complete the rest of the pilgrimage.

Utsumi, who had been in training on Hiei since he was fourteen years old, was in excellent condition and breezed through the first five 100-day terms. Quite unexpectedly in the middle of the sixth term, he was stricken with terrible intestinal cramps, suffering from severe diarrhea for a week. Dehydrated and racked with pain and fever, Utsumi took nearly twenty hours to drag himself over a course he would normally run through in six or seven hours. Near death, he collapsed on the floor of his room. Just then his master made a surprise visit.

"Get up and get out on the road! A *gyōja* must walk regardless of his condition!" Kakushō yelled at his prostrate disciple.

Utsumi staggered out into the gloom, and when he arrived at Shaka-dō, one of the main stations of worship, hours behind schedule, he found one of his master's attendants standing in front of the temple. "The master waited here for you from midnight but then had to return to his temple to conduct the morning service. He left me with instructions to give you this medicinal drink."

Utsumi took the medicine and partially revived. At this stage, Utsumi has said, he forgot about himself, entrusting his life to Fudō Myō-ō and moving along under a higher power. He went on to safely finish the term. (Utsumi has, in common with the other marathon monks, amazing recuperative powers. During a physical examination before his twelve-year retreat, his doctor, looking at an X-ray of the monk's stomach, said, "I see that you had a duodenal ulcer." "I did?" Utsumi exclaimed—during his novice days, Utsumi had developed and then cured himself of a "bad stomach ache.")

Later, Utsumi was shocked to hear rumors that other priests on Hiei were saying that the reason he got so sick was his lack of intensity and his perfunctory performance of the ritual—Fudō was "punishing" the cocky monk for insufficient sincerity. This made Utsumi determined to redeem himself during *dōiri*. He remained perfectly erect throughout the long ordeal, and unlike all the other *gyōja*,

Utsumi, razor-sharp on the fourth day of *dōiri*. ▶

who were carried out of the hall and down the stairs on the shoulders of their attendants, Utsumi strode gallantly out of Myō-ō-dō under his own power. When he was pronounced a Tōgyōman Ajari and received the medicinal *hō-no-yū* drink, Utsumi felt "as if the entire universe was mine; all was serene and my mind was clear and bright."

Utsumi completed the full 1,000-day term in 1979 and the 100,000-prayer, eight-day fast and fire ceremony in 1981. He succeeded his master as abbot of Myō-ō-dō, the mecca of *kaihōgyō* practitioners, shortly thereafter.

Utsumi is likely the most approachable of all the modern *kaihōgyōja*. Dozens of people visit Myō-ō-dō each day to seek his advice, attend the fire ceremony, join him for lunch, or copy sutras under his direction. The friendly, outgoing priest enjoys meeting foreigners and has guided a number of them over the course. He established "one-day *kaihōgyō*" training sessions open to all twice a month from spring to summer.

To be sure, Utsumi is razor-sharp mentally and physically, but he is not a harsh or forbidding person; indeed, he radiates a contagious *joie de vivre*. He enjoys smoking and likes, in the off-season, to walk down to the main complex of Enryaku-ji to drink a cup of coffee in the restaurant there and flirt with the pretty young waitresses. In Japan it is the custom for girls to present chocolates to boys on Valentine's Day, and once when I was in Utsumi's room he pointed with pride at the big pile of chocolates in the corner—"Too bad they are all 'obligation' sweets," he joked. ("Obligation" sweets are those presented to one's male relatives, teachers, or bosses.) He is a fine scholar who can discuss the intricacies of Buddhism with anyone but loves to tease academics, both Japanese and foreign: "Study is fine, but if you really want to know what Buddhism is all about, do *kaihōgyō* with me."

Several years ago, the energetic Utsumi took up ping-pong, playing the game with the same intensity he gives *kaihōgyō*. Not surprisingly, he has become quite proficient at table tennis, and he loves to issue a challenge to all comers. He has engaged several top-ranked players with increasingly good results. His favorite tactic is to take his opponent on *kaihōgyō* and then have a match: if the game lasts long enough Utsumi can win, for he never tires!

Utsumi shares the other Ajaris' love for baseball. High school baseball is a religion in Japan, and Utsumi helped coach the Hiei High School team for several

◄ Utsumi emerging from Myō-ō-dō upon completion of *dōiri:* a new Buddhist saint is born.

years when he was a trainee monk. One year the team emerged victorious in the extremely competitive play-off rounds in the Kyoto area and qualified for the national tournament. Utsumi was ecstatic and accompanied the team to Ōsaka, where he was given, for the first and probably the last time in his life, meat and po-tatoes. His team was eliminated—"the low point in my career as a Tendai priest," he jokes—and shortly thereafter he decided to undergo the *sennichi kaihōgyō*.

Utsumi once told me: "If the subject is baseball, I can talk for hours and my audience will listen to every word, but if I pontificate about 'Buddhism' or 'train-ing,' their eyes glaze over in twenty minutes. Those things must be experienced firsthand, and words simply cannot convey what they mean. Therefore, I try to stick to topics that my parishioners and visitors can understand, relating Buddhist truths in an entertaining manner, letting them absorb Tendai naturally from these sur-roundings, their participation in the fire ceremony, and *kaihōgyō*."

A typical day for Utsumi as abbot of Myō-ō-dō begins with an hour-long morning service at 6:00 A.M. Afterward he gives instructions to the trainee monks outlining the day's chores, and he, in turn, is informed of incoming messages and worshipers and guests expected later on. Following a simple breakfast, Utsumi practices calligraphy, answers letters, and takes care of other temple business. Around 10:00 A.M. worshipers begin arriving for the morning fire ceremony; Utsumi generally greets them over tea. The number of participants can range from a handful during the week to over a hundred on Sundays and national holidays. The worshipers write their petitions on prayer sticks, which are consumed during the fire ceremony.

The fire ceremony lasts little over an hour, ending with a long group recitation of the Fudō Myō-ō *mantra*. In conclusion, Utsumi comes out to bless the people in the hall with a touch of his rosary. Everyone is then invited in for a delicious vegetarian lunch. Unlike the delicate vegetarian fare of Kyoto restaurants, the meals served at Myō-ō-dō are rich and hearty. (Utsumi, who acted for years as cook when he was a trainee, grades each dish, giving his disciples pointers on how to improve the taste.)

Top. Every day Utsumi performs the Tendai fire ceremony (*goma*) at Myō-ō-dō. During this ancient rite, the celebrant calls forth the countless deities of the Vedic, Buddhist, Taoist, Shinto, and folk god pantheons and then consumes them with the fiery wisdom of Fudō. The monk casts everything he has into the flames, leaving nothing behind, to totally identify with Fudō Myō-ō. Once that is accomplished, the monk is capable, it is believed, of channeling Fudō's power to others. ▶

Bottom. Utsumi leading a group of one-day marathon monks. Everyone is welcome! ▶

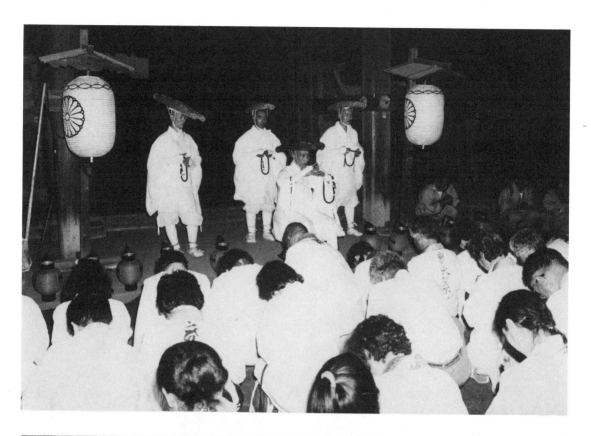

During the meal, Utsumi chats easily with his guests, more often than not discussing baseball with them, and listening sympathetically to any personal problems that may come up. There is another fire ceremony at 2:00 P.M., and Utsumi spends the rest of the afternoon meeting with other guests, playing ping-pong, and inspecting the temple grounds. There is an evening service at 6:00, followed by a light dinner and a leisurely bath. Utsumi usually retires around nine, although he sometimes stays up to talk with worshipers staying the night.

In addition to the twice-a-day fire ceremony, Utsumi conducts a monthly sutra-copying session, twice-monthly "one-day *kaihōgyō*" from April to October, and a summer "camp" for schoolchildren, many of whom are physically or mentally handicapped. Also in summer, high school track and field clubs come to Myō-ō-dō to train by doing *kaihōgyō* and running up and down the hundreds of stone steps on Hiei. Utsumi loves to join in the training, racing the young atheletes to the top of the stairs—he almost always wins and eventually runs them ragged.

There are special four-day fasts and fire ceremonies from December 31 to January 3 and in mid-November. Utsumi further sponsors a Great Marathon for his parishioners, usually in June. On the day of the Great Marathon, Utsumi's parishioners assemble at Sekisan-in at 4:00 A.M. They accompany the monk and one or two of his disciples on a 50-kilometer (33-mile) run around Kyoto. In addition to all the regular stops on the Great Marathon, Utsumi visits the homes or businesses of fifteen or so of his parishioners along the way. The stops typically include a visit to a bank president's villa, a traditional geisha teahouse, a seafood restaurant, several shops, and the homes of ordinary working folk. At each stop, the group tagging along Utsumi is treated to tea, cool drinks, and snacks while the monk conducts a short service inside. As the procession winds its way through Kyoto, an attendant monk blows on a conch shell to alert the residents. People rush out into the street to be blessed. Even boys playing baseball in the park will interrupt their game to be touched on the head by the marathon monk's rosary and, not incidentally, receive the candy that a trailing attendant hands out.

The marathon ends at around 11:00 P.M. at Sekizan-in, but the fact that there are many rest stops enables a large percentage of the parishioners, ranging in age

◄ *Top.* Utsumi blessing the crowd at the last stop of the One-Day Run through Kyoto. Many of the parishioners have accompanied the Ajari for the entire 54-kilometer run.

◄ *Bottom.* Utsumi takes a well-deserved break at Kiyomizu-dera during the Great Marathon of 84 kilometers, run for 100 consecutive days. Despite the severity of the trial, Utsumi has a smile for his parishioners.

from ten to over seventy, to complete the entire circuit. (Others drop out or join halfway.)

With generous supporters all over the nation—as many as 50,000 parishioners according to one account—and substantial donations from the stream of visitors who visit each day, Myō-ō-dō has become a wealthy temple. Utsumi uses the money wisely, supporting as many as a dozen trainee monks and lay attendants and providing nearly eight hundred meals a month to his visitors. One of Utsumi's lay attendants, a former nightclub entertainer, made a name for himself by performing informal *kaihōgyō* every day, summer and winter, for three years.

Utsumi's twelve-year retreat was up in March 1987. His chief disciple, Tanno Kakudō, is currently performing *sennichi kaihōgyō,* and Utsumi evidently hopes to appoint the monk as his successor. Once there is a new abbot of Myō-ō-dō, Utsumi appears to want to descend from the mountain, after thirty years of training, and return to the world below.

If ever there was an unlikely candidate for Buddhahood it was Sakai Yūsai, the ninth *sennichi kaihōgyō* of the modern era.[7] Sakai was born in Ōsaka in 1926, the eldest son of a family that eventually contained ten children. His father was a rice merchant, and when he went bankrupt speculating in the grain market the family moved to Tokyo, where they lived hand to mouth for some years.

Sakai's relatives and friends remember him as something of a crybaby, a sleepy-head, and a very dull student. He was, by all accounts, unexceptional, although the family recalls that he was never attached to his possessions—if he won at marbles, he would immediately return his winnings to the loser, and he would give away his pencils or toys without hesitation to his brothers and sisters if they asked for them.

Following elementary school, Sakai enrolled in night school and worked at a military hospital laboratory to help support his family. (He later learned to his dismay that the lab specialized in the production of chemicals for germ warfare.) The family financial situation worsened when Sakai's father was drafted, despite his large number of dependents, and sent to the front in China, where he was seriously wounded. Sakai was so hungry at this time that he often stole and ate the feed for the lab animals. The teachers at Sakai's school informed him that because of poor attendance and low marks he could never graduate as a regular student. The only option open to the failing student was to enlist in the army, which would guarantee automatic graduation. Sakai did so, and in 1944, he was assigned to a naval base in

Kagoshima, Japan's southernmost island—an area exposed to the full wrath of the American air force.

By that time Japan had lost the war for all practical purposes, and few of the pilots in Sakai's division returned from their futile sorties. American bombers from Okinawa began raiding Sakai's base, raking it daily with machine-gun fire and bombs. As soon as Sakai and the rest of the ground crew repaired the runways, they would be attacked again. The death of his comrades and the futility of war anguished the young soldier: "Why have so many fine men perished while a no-account like me remains alive?" Japan surrendered in August 1945; the men at Sakai's base were told that the war effort had been "suspended" and they were all to return home. The transportation system had been largely destroyed, and it took Sakai nearly a month to make it back to Tokyo.

When he reached the desolate city, Sakai found his family alive, but everything else had been lost in the firebombing. He found a job as a clerk in the Hosei University library and worked quietly there for two years. He and his father then opened up a noodle shop in an entertainment district; the shop prospered, and they also did brisk business selling daily necessities, at the time in very short supply, on the side. Sakai procured those items on the black market. Tragedy struck when fire in the neighborhood engulfed their restaurant. They were unable to rebuild the business, and Sakai became a full-time black-marketeer. He did well for himself on occasion but ultimately lost his shirt in the panic of 1954.

Thereafter, Sakai aimlessly drifted from job to job. He married a cousin, but the shy, retiring girl adjusted poorly to the match—within a month of the wedding, she returned to her family's home in Ōsaka. Sakai quit his job in Tokyo and rejoined his wife in Ōsaka. He was unable to learn the nature of his wife's discontent, and she seemed to improve. Two months later, however, she killed herself.

Shattered, Sakai lived purposelessly, working as a shipwright in a large boatyard. When he was thirty-five years old, one of his aunts took along her listless nephew on a visit to Hiei. At first Sakai thought to himself, "Why on earth did she drag me to this awful place?" Yet he was also strangely attracted to the quiet on the mountain and the stately demeanor of the priests, perhaps remembering past visions of his grandfather, whom he had once seen dressed up in full *yamabushi* regalia.

On his days off, Sakai would wander around Hiei. On one such occasion he saw Miyamoto Ichijō emerge from Myō-ō-dō on the last day of *dōiri,* an impression that remains with him to this day. After learning about the practice of *kaihōgyō,* Sakai began doing informal pilgrimages in the Ōsaka area near his home and occasionally making the return trip from Hiei to Ōsaka on foot, a good 50-kilometer hike. One day Sakai decided to ask Kobayashi Ryūshō, a Hiei priest he greatly admired, to accept him as a lay monk on a month's trial basis. Such a request is not at all unusual on Hiei, a kind of last hope for unrepentant sinners. At the same time there was a furniture dealer at Kobayashi's temple who had been sent there by his family to cure him of habitual gambling. Kobayashi took both lost souls in, and the two men helped out with temple chores—chopping wood, cleaning the grounds, preparing meals, and attending the services. Near the end of the month-long trial the two lay monks secluded themselves in the temple and chanted the names of the three thousand Buddhas, each recitation accompanied by a full prostration. The gambler, cured of his affliction, returned happily to Kyoto, but Sakai wished to remain on the mountain. Kobayashi felt that Sakai was different from the other troubled souls who worked out their problems with a dose of Tendai practice and agreed to sponsor the forty-year-old for ordination. Sakai, the man who—in his own words—"had experienced hell," became a Tendai priest at the end of 1965.

Kobayashi sent Sakai to do his initial training under one of his disciples, Ōdera Bunei, head priest of Reizan-in. Ōdera, seven years Sakai's junior, was a dedicated scholar-priest. As a young monk he had studied in Burma for two years, following the Theravādin rule, the only priest from Hiei to finish the two-year term. The one-time dunce Sakai was inspired by the example of Ōdera, a recognized expert in Tendai thought, who stayed up late every evening poring over his books after a full day of conducting temple business.

A novice monk is a novice monk regardless of his age, and Sakai cheerfully fulfilled the tasks required of newcomers. He cleaned, shopped, cooked, and helped tend Ōdera's five little children (including a pair of twins), taking them to the park to play, feeding them, and changing their diapers. Sakai's family, with the exception of his grandfather the *yamabushi* priest, had never been religious, and they were all shocked to learn that their relative was acting as a temple servant without pay.

Sakai enrolled in the Hiei Higher Academy in 1966 and, in a miraculous

Top. Sakai, at 1:30 A.M., getting ready to take off on a 40-kilometer run. ▶
Bottom. Sakai speeding along the marathon monk route in Imuro Valley. Every day he covers from 40 to 84 kilometers, dashing up and down temple steps, leaping across mountain streams, and bounding through dense forests. ▶

turnabout, passed both the basic and advanced course with honors. In fact, his graduation thesis, "Dengyō Daishi's Theory of Gods and Buddhas," won the "Abbot's Award" as the best student essay of that year.

In 1971 Sakai embarked on a three-year retreat in order to qualify as a head priest of one of the temples on Hiei. The following year he completed his first 100-day term of *kaihōgyō* and then decided to attempt the 90-day ceaseless *nembutsu*. Uncharacteristically, Sakai did not consult with either Kobayashi or Ōdera before submitting his petition to Enryaku-ji headquarters. When they heard of the plan, both opposed it because of Sakai's advanced age and the severity of the practice. One monk in the nineteenth century had attempted the ceaseless *nembutsu;* his legs swelled to twice their normal size, he collapsed in the training hall, and he died a week later with these words: "Please, please do not let anyone do this anymore."

Since that time there had been no candidates for the practice until Sakai and a classmate at the Hiei Higher Academy, Takagawa Jishō, applied. Like most of the top *gyōja,* Takagawa came from general society rather than a temple family, entering Mount Hiei at age twenty. After much discussion among the senior priests, permission was granted to the aspirants. From June 1 to August 30 Sakai and Takagawa were sequestered at the twin temples of Jōgyō-dō and Hokke-dō.

The ceaseless *nembutsu* involves constant revolution around the hall while chanting endlessly, "Hail to Amida Buddha, Hail to Amida Buddha." In the beginning, Sakai felt as if he were walking on air gliding around the hall; later it was if he were traipsing through deep mud. He slept poorly in the two hours of rest-meditation that he was allowed each day, and during the walking he sometimes lost consciousness temporarily and fell asleep against the railing for five minutes or so. Near the end of the ninety-day term Sakai perceived himself moving along a narrow white path over a raging river. Even though he was revolving around a square room, Sakai distinctly sensed himself walking in a straight line as the path opened before him. The ghosts and goblins that had previously threatened him turned into the Buddhas and Bodhisattvas of the *Lotus Sūtra,* and all was peace and light. Sakai recalls reposing in a timeless state, one with Amida Buddha.

Kobayashi, concerned about Sakai's condition, frequently visited the training hall during the night to check on his disciple. He was surprised that Sakai's voice was consistently stronger than that of Takagawa's next door, even though the other monk was twenty-one years younger.

In 1974 Sakai finished his three-year retreat and went to Tokyo to call on his ailing father. He also made a pilgrimage to Buddhist holy sites in India. After his return to Hiei and assumption of the position of abbot of Hōjū-in, Sakai resolved to undertake *sennichi kaihōgyō*. Since he was intent on selecting the hardest course, he petitioned the demanding master Hakozaki to accept him as the restorer of Imuro Valley *sennichi kaihōgyō*.

Hakozaki was the harshest taskmaster on Hiei; in addition, Chōjū-in was an isolated place with few visitors to break the monotony. Consequently, none of Hakozaki's previous disciples had lasted more than a few months on the job—even the exemplary Ōdera had to call it quits in less than half a year. One unsuccessful postulant recalls working with Hakozaki in the fields: one day Hakozaki nearly severed his toe with the sharp hoe, but he refused to stop until all the work was done. The sight of the abbot's bloody toe, attached to his foot by a sliver of flesh, flapping back and forth, was more than the young trainee could bear, and he fled the temple. Normally Sakai would have been spared regular temple duty as a Hiei abbot, but since he was the only other monk at Chōjū-in, he was obliged to act as Hakozaki's attendant.

As mentioned above, Hakozaki had restored the Imuro Valley course in 1943 and conducted a 100-day *kaihōgyō* term there. Another monk, named Ōtsuka, did a 100-day term over the course in 1970 or 1971, and Sakai began his effort to permanently reestablish the Imuro Valley course in 1975. Hakozaki was then too old (age eighty-two) to take Sakai around the course, so Ōtsuka and Miyamoto Ichijō, who had been entrusted with Hakozaki's maps and charts, went over the route with him. Sakai was forced to make a few alterations because portions of the course had been completely washed away by flash floods or blocked by new road construction. Sakai began his 1,000-day pilgrimage on April 7, coincidentally the birthday of his master Hakozaki and the anniversary of his wife's death. Hakozaki's advice: "Ever onward; never look back."

On top of his daily *kaihōgyō* of 40-kilometers, Sakai had to handle all of the cleaning, cooking, and laundry for the two of them. He rose each day at midnight, purified himself in the temple's two waterfalls, conducted the morning service, and then set out on *kaihōgyō* around 1:30 A.M. Upon his return to Chōjū-in at around 8:30, he attended to all the chores. Under normal circumstances, Sakai would have been able to retire around 8:00 P.M., but Hakozaki was, at the time, in the habit of taking a nightcap, and Sakai, of course, had to heat and serve the sake. Word got out that the exuberant Hakozaki was treating guests to copious amounts of rice wine; consequently, almost every night parishioners showed up to keep the old master company. Sakai was on duty until the final visitor staggered home, and after cleaning up he barely had time for an hour or two of sleep.

Sakai has said that of all the trials he has undergone, the first two years at Chōjū-in were by far the worst. Hakozaki was deliberately testing Sakai's mettle—like all true masters, he wanted his disciple to surpass him—and the old priest gave Sakai no rest. When Sakai, for instance, began to prepare meals in advance to save a few precious moments, Hakozaki rejected the food with a curt "This is stale!" Sometimes when he did prostrations in the temple, Sakai was so tired that he would fall fast asleep as he touched his head to the floor. Sakai was so sure that he would die of exhaustion on the route that he began to carry the equivalent of several hundred dollars in cash on his person rather than the customary symbolic few cents as consolation money for whoever discovered his body and arranged for his funeral.

Sakai survived, and during the fourth 100-day term he achieved a break-through—he was no longer troubled by visions of his dead wife and army pals or other distracting and disturbing thoughts, nor was he tormented by physical and spiritual pain. He successfully completed *dōiri,* with most of his family in attendance on the last day, and seemed to be safely on his way to finishing the full 1,000-day term.

The path of *gyōja* is never completely smooth, however. About a week before setting out on the Sekisan Marathon, Sakai was doing preliminary training in the mountains when he was attacked by a wild boar. There had been piles of snow on Hiei that winter, and the boar, a touchy beast anyway, was probably starving and thus charged the monk in a furious attempt to drive away a perceived threat to its food supply. As Sakai leaped out of the way, he was either slashed by the boar's tusks or lacerated by a sharp branch. Sakai ignored the wound, but it soon festered, and after a few days of Sekisan Marathon his first two toes had swollen to twice their normal size and turned deep purple.

Once a monk has completed a 1,000-day marathon, he is acclaimed a Buddhist saint of the highest order. Most of the monks keep on running, but at a more leisurely pace, delightfully sporting in the practice. On his runs these days, the veteran Sakai will stop at temples along the way to have a cup of tea and a cookie, and chat with the priest and his family. One temple wife says of Sakai's visits, "It makes my day; he is always so fresh and bright." ▶

The toenail on his big toe had fallen off, and the pain was so intense that he shrieked in pain with each step. Unable to continue, Sakai sat down on a rock on an isolated spot, pulled out his "suicide knife," and lanced the wound; blood and pus gushed out, and Sakai fell into a faint. He pointed the knife at his throat so that if he fell the blade would pierce the skin and he would remain faithful to his vow to kill himself if he failed to complete the course. Thirty minutes later, the groggy monk recovered slightly from the shock, wiped off the wound, and proceeded to Sekisan-in, where a crowd of believers awaited his arrival. Showing up at the temple gates an hour late, Sakai apologized for the delay, explaining sheepishly that he had "over-slept." Sakai washed off the wound again with temple well water, rested a bit, and then started back on the return trip. Out of sight of the believers, he fainted again but recovered in about ten minutes. Sakai knew now that he was tapping a higher power just as he had been at the darkest moments of the ceaseless *nembutsu* practice. Reliance on human strength was out of the question; Sakai felt he must have been propelled along by a superior force.

Even though the injury never healed properly for the duration of Sekisan Marathon, Sakai miraculously completed the term. Another Hiei priest heard the story and walked by the place where Sakai had lanced his wound; he nearly passed out at the sight of the blood- and pus-splattered rock. Following this incident, Sakai truly earned the respect of his master Hakozaki, and the old priest presented Sakai with this *haiku:*

> The path of practice:
> Where will be
> My final resting place?

According to the oldest documents, the last three terms should be conducted in the traditional manner, that is, from Mudō-ji Valley, and Sakai conducted the remaining terms from his former temple of Hōjū-in. As mentioned previously, the actual number of days on the road usually comes to 975 or 980 because of the time out for the Katsuragawa Summer Retreat. Sakai, ever the innovator, wished to do a full 1,000 days, so after the official ceremony of *dosoku sandai,* he logged twenty-five more days at Imuro Valley.

Sakai has often expressed his desire to die on the road, and not long after finishing the first 1,000-day term in 1980, he went for a second. This time he

Sakai emerging from the woods. When asked once what frightened him the most during his runs—darkness? wild animals? apparitions?—he replied: "People! They think that I am a ghost and let out terrible screams."

finished in six years: 200 days the first and second years, 100 the third, 200 the fourth, 100 the fifth, and 200 the sixth. He came out of his second *dōiri* in better shape than the first. (It is said that the liquid spat back into the cup during *dōiri* is usually dark brown and foul-smelling. In Sakai's case, the second time it was pure white.) The second 1,000-day term was very close to the Buddhist ideal of "Every day is a good day." On day 2,000 films of the sixty-one-year-old marvel zooming along the mountain paths were shown on every television news program in Japan. Looking tan and ever so fit, the supermonk announced his intention to realize his dream of *kaihōgyō* to the sacred mountains of China. Sakai did complain, however, about the increased pollution of Kyoto's air: "During the second Great Marathon I nearly choked on the smog, which was much worse than before." He completed the 100,000-prayer fire ceremony and nine-day fast in 1983 and plans another in 1988.

During the *kaihōgyō* terms, Sakai typically sleeps from 9:00 P.M. to midnight. Upon rising he heads straight for the two waterfalls of Chōjū-in, where he purifies

The marathon monks, known as the "white cranes of Hiei," have been flying above the clouds for over a thousand years.

himself in each one for a few minutes while chanting the Fudō Myō-o *mantra*. (Sakai began waterfall training the day after he witnessed the blind and lame Hakozaki enter the falls in midwinter.) He then conducts a forty-minute service in the temple and sets off around 1:10 A.M., arriving back at around 9:00 A.M. On non-*kaihōgyō* days, Sakai rises at 2:30 for waterfall purification, conducts the service, and then takes one or the other of his dogs for a long walk in the mountains.

When Sakai completed his first 1,000-day term, Hakozaki retired at age eighty-nine, turning over Chōjū-in to his one and only prize disciple. Hakozaki and Sakai are alike in many ways. Both men became monks around age forty following stormy careers in the world below. Seemingly in an effort to make up for the wasted first half of their lives, they threw themselves into their training and, in terms of accomplishments, they rank as two of the greatest monks who ever practiced on Hiei or anywhere else in the Buddhist world. Sakai refers to Kobayashi and Ōdera (who passed away at the young age of fifty-two) as his teachers but always calls Hakozaki "Grandfather."

The continually smiling Sakai is rather less intimidating than the gruff Hakozaki and more approachable, a wonderful combination of intensity and warmth. The long years of training and ceaseless introspection have rubbed the rough edges smooth, and Sakai is—as one would expect of a living Buddha—open, wise, and unpretentious. His sanctity is unsanctimonious; constantly smiling—even just before *dōiri,* the "living death"—Sakai unostentatiously makes tea for his guests while chatting away in a lively Ōsaka accent, answers the phone with a hearty "Hello, this is Sakai," and slips into a threadbare warmup suit when he has a lot of calligraphy to brush. One of Sakai's favorite calligraphic sayings is the Zen-flavored "Everyday mind is the way." Sakai never boasts of mystic flights or clairvoyant powers; the only unusual experience he might mention is the breaking of his rosary at the moment of his father's death in a Tokyo hospital.

One unique quality about Sakai is his sensitivity to all forms of life. As he walked through the mountains day after day, he was struck by the incredible energy of the weeds, how they sprout and grow despite all obstacles. Even though weeding is an important Buddhist practice, Sakai stopped weeding his temple garden, explaining: "Weeds, too, have a right to live." This marathon monk is also fond of animals. The beasts he encounters on his runs—birds, rabbits, monkeys, deer, snakes, even boars—he feels are his companions. Sakai keeps a bunch of dogs at his temple, including a couple of real old mongrels, and at least one happily wags along with its master on the *kaihōgyō* rounds.

Regarding his practice, Sakai has said: "Human life is like a candle; if it burns out halfway it does no one any good. I want the flame of my practice to consume my candle completely, letting that light illuminate thousands of places. My practice is to live wholeheartedly, with gratitude and without regret. Practice really has no beginning nor end; when practice and daily life are one, that is true Buddhism."

This effervescent sixty-year-old marathon monk often exclaims brightly to his visitors, "Life is so wonderful!"

Among the fifty or so priests who have completed a 100-day *kaihōgyō* term since 1868, Hiramatsu Chōku is one of the most interesting. A former military man who served in both Japan's Imperial Army and the postwar Self-Defense Force, Hiramatsu became a Tendai priest shortly after his retirement from the force at age fifty-four. He enrolled in a Buddhist university and then decided to undergo a 100-day *kaihōgyō.* Since he was in excellent shape and accustomed to hardship as a military officer, the Hiei Council of Gyōja granted him permission despite his advanced age and recent ordination. He is also the only priest (it is thought) to have been married while performing the marathon.

Hiramatsu completed the 100-day term successfully in 1979, not without quite of bit of difficulty because of sore legs. The soldier-turned-priest published his *Diary of a Kaihōgyō Monk* in 1981.[8] The account is matter-of-fact, devoid of any mystical flights or profound realizations—Hiramatsu thought mostly of his dead war buddies during his rounds and confessed sheepishly that on one particularly muggy day he thought to himself en route, "A cold beer would really hit the spot right now." He was also embarrassed that people frequently mistook him for Sakai—they are about the same age—and asked for a blessing. Hiramatsu later published his master's thesis, *Research on Kaihōgyō,* and then completed studies for a Ph.D.

Other *kaihōgyō* monks have dispersed to various parts of Japan, carrying with them the wisdom acquired from the practice; a few have gone overseas to, for example, live a mendicant life in India, study at an American college, or teach in Europe. One Tendai professor-priest has set up a *kaihōgyō* course on California's Mount Tamalipis, a sacred American Indian site. A young monk from India who was raised on Mount Hiei between the ages of ten and twenty-five did a 100-day *kaihōgyō* term. Recently he has returned to his native land to propagate Tendai Buddhism.

Over the years, a variety of non-Japanese have, for brief periods, tagged along with the marathon monks on their runs. When he was living in Kyoto, Walter Nowick, a pianist and Zen teacher currently based in the United States, frequently accompanied Hagami on his rounds. More recently, a high school student from a U.S. army base in Japan has spent his summer vacations walking with Utsumi.

Theoretically, a woman could undertake the 100-day *kaihōgyō,* but formal permission is not likely to be granted anytime soon owing to the recent failure of a young Japanese Jōdo sect nun to finish a preliminary 21-day term, being forced to quit on the twentieth day because of exhaustion. A spunky middle-aged American woman who hopes someday to complete ten 100-day terms over ten years also failed in her initial attempt; she was forced to give up after about three weeks because of sore legs. (Reportedly she is in hard training for another crack at the route). Sooner or later, a non-Japanese *gyōja,* male or female, is sure to appear on the scene and Hiei will then have its first international 1,000-day marathon monk or nun.

Epilogue

THE MARATHON MONKS are splendid atheletes to be sure, and the severity of their training defies belief, but to me the most admirable thing about the Hiei *gyōja* is their warmth, open-heartedness, and humanity—qualities far more important than the ability to run 1,000 marathons in a seven-year period. Tendai training has brought out the best in each of the monks, pushing to the surface the wonderful Buddha-nature we all possess deep within but rarely manifest. Facing death over and over, the marathon monks become alive to each moment, full of gratitude, joy, and grace.

Since all of us are on pilgrimage in one manner or the other, the marathon monks of Hiei have much to teach us about treading the Path: always aim for the ultimate, never look back, be mindful of others at all times, and keep the mind forever set on the Way. "If you do this," the marathon monks are telling us, "there is nothing that cannot be accomplished."

Notes

THE TREASURE OF A NATION

1. These are the most famous words of Saichō, taught to every Japanese schoolchild. They form the introduction to his celebrated work *Sange-gakushō-shiki* (or, as it is usually called, *Rokujō-shiki*). "Mind set on the Way" is *dōshin* (Skt. *bodhicitta*), the consciousness that seeks awakening. There has been a great deal of controversy regarding the proper interpretation of sentence five. Due to a copyist's error the line was reprinted for centuries in Tendai manuals as "One who illuminates his own corner." That phrase, unfortunately, was selected as the motto of a movement to improve society initiated by the Tendai sect some years ago, and embarrassed senior officials are reluctant to admit that the wording is, strictly speaking, incorrect. The translation given here is based on the original manuscript in Saichō's own hand and the Chinese tale behind the quotation. For further discussion of the problem, including a translation of the Chinese tale, see Paul Groner, *Saichō* (Berkeley: Berkeley Buddhist Series 7, 1984), pp. 116–117, and Sonoda Kōyū, "Genjitsu kōtei no tetsugaku," in *Tendai-shū* (Tokyo: Shogakukan 1986), pp. 52–54.

2. The year of Saichō's birth and the correct name of his parents, too, have been points of academic debate recently (Groner, pp. 19–21). Although Saichō's birth date is traditionally given as 767 and his father's name as being Momo-e, Hirakawa Akira maintains that modern scholarship has proven conclusively that Saichō was in fact born in 766 and that his father's name was actually Kiyoshi: Hirakawa Akira, *Saichō* (Tokyo: Shūeisha, 1985) pp. 31–35. Saichō's mother was thought to have been one Fujiwara Tōshi, but doubts about this have also surfaced.

3. Groner's book is the only full-length study of Saichō in English. There is an outdated biography of Saichō in Bruno Petzold's *Tendai Buddhism* (Tokyo: International Buddhist Exchange Center, 1979) pp. 135–165. Among the dozens of biographies and studies of Saichō in Japanese the following are recommended: the huge *Dengyō daishi kenkyū* (Tokyo: Waseda Daigaku Shuppan-bu, 1973) contains essays on every aspect of Saichō's life and thought; Sonoda Kōyū and Andō Toshio, *Saichō* (Tokyo: Iwanami Shoten, 1974); Kiuchi Hiroshi, *Dengyō daishi no shōgai to shisō* (Tokyo: Daisan-bunmeisha, 1976); Watanabe Shujun, *Saichō no kokoro to shōgai* (Tokyo: Yūzankaku, 1977); Shiori Ryōdō and Kiuchi Gyō-ō (eds.), *Saichō* (Tokyo: Yoshikawa Kobunkan, 1982), which contains many interesting essays;

Hirakawa Akira *Saichō* (Tokyo: Shūseisha, 1985); Umebara Takeshi, *Saichō Meisō* (Tokyo, Kōsei Shuppansha, 1987); and Nagai Michiko, *Saichō o tadoru* (Tokyo: Kōdansha, 1987).

4. Takasaki Jikidō (ed.), *Acta Asiatica*, no. 47 (Tokyo: Tōhō Gakkai, 1985), p. 2. This issue of *Acta Asiatica*, "The Assimilation of Buddhism in Ancient Japan: From Introduction to Firm Acceptance," is the most comprehensive study of early Japanese Buddhism. The best survey of the entire spectrum of Buddhism in Japan is Daigan and Alicia Matsunaga's *Foundations of Japanese Buddhism,* vols. 1 and 2 (Los Angeles and Tokyo: Buddhist Books International, 1974–1976). Other studies of Japanese Buddhism are Marius W. De Visser, *Ancient Buddhism in Japan* (Leiden: E. J. Brill, 1935); E. Steinilber-Oberlin, *The Buddhist Sects of Japan* (London: Allen & Unwin, 1938); Sir Charles Eliot, *Japanese Buddhism,* (London: Edward Arnold, 1939); Watanabe Shōkō, *Japanese Buddhism* (Tokyo: Japanese Cultural Society, 1970); and Dale E. Saunders, *Buddhism in Japan* (Tokyo: Tuttle, 1972).

5. The teachings of the Six Schools of Nara Buddhism are covered in painstaking detail in Matsunaga, vol. 1, pp. 28–109. See also Junjirō Takakusa, *The Essentials of Buddhist Philosophy* (Honolulu: University of Hawaii Press, 1956).

6. A quotation from Saichō's *Kanshō Tendai nembun gakushō-shiki (Hachijō-shiki).* For a translation of this work see Groner, pp. 131–135.

7. The complete works of Saichō, *Dengyō daishi zenshū,* have been published in five volumes, the latest edition by the Nihon Bussho Kankō-kai in 1975. The *Ganmon* is the opening work of volume 1. A detailed commentary in Japanese on the *Ganmon* is found in Hirakawa, pp. 71–109.

8. It is interesting to note that the Four Great Vows, now a prominent feature of Zen ceremonies, originated with the Tendai school. The vows are as follows: "Sentient beings are innumerable but still I vow to save them all. Passions are inexhaustible but still I vow to cut them off. Dharma teachings are unlimited but still I vow to master each one. The Buddhist Way is supreme but still I vow to attain it."

9. Both texts are available in English translation: Yoshito Hakeda, *The Awakening of Faith* (New York: Columbia University Press, 1967), and Thomas Cleary, *The Flower Ornament Scripture,* 3 vols. (Boston and London: Shambhala Publications, 1984–1987).

10. For further information on Chih-i see Leon Hurvitz, *Chih-i* (Brussels: Melanges et Bouddhiques No. 12, 1960–1962).

11. The famous Chinese Ch'an eccentrics Han-shan and Shih-te (Jap. Kanzan and Jittoku) lived on T'ien-t'ai. See Burton Watson (trans.), *Cold Mountain* (New York: Columbia University Press, 1970).

12. English translations of the *Lotus Sutra,* in order of readability, are : Bunnō Katō et al., *The Threefold Lotus Sutra* (Tokyo and New York: Weatherhill/Kōsei, 1975); Leon Hurvitz, *Scripture of the Lotus Blossom of the Fine Dharma* (New York: Columbia University Press, 1976); Senchū Murano, *The Lotus Sutra* (Tokyo: Nichiren-Shu Headquarters, 1974). For a translation of the Chinese text of the *Nirvāṇa Sūtra* see Yamamoto Kōshō, *The Mahāyāna Mahāparinirvāṇa Sūtra,* 3 vols. (Ube: Karinbunko, 1973–1975).

13. For detailed explanations of classical T'ien-t'ai thought see David W. Chappell (ed.), *T'ien-t'ai Buddhism: An Outline of the Fourfold Teachings* (Tokyo: Daiichi-Shobō, 1983); Petzold, pp. 1–70; and Matsunaga, pp. 152–56.

14. The manual is available in English translation by Charles Luk (Lu K'uan Yu), *The Secrets of Chinese Meditation* (York Beach, Maine: Samuel Weiser, 1969) pp. 109–62. An easy-to-follow commentary on the edition of the text used in Japan is found in Sekiguchi Shindai, *Tendai shōshikan* (Tokyo: Daitō Shuppansha, 1978).

15. *Dengyō daishi zenshū*, vol. 4, pp. 281–284. See also two books by Yamada Etai: *Hokke-kyō to dengyō daishi* (Tokyo: Daiichi-Shobō, 1973) and *Dōshin wa kuni no takara* (Tokyo: Kōsei Shuppansha, 1987). These two books by the present *zasu* (supreme abbot) of Hiei reflect the current emphasis in Tendai on the Lotus Buddhism of Saichō.

16. R. H. Blyth, *Zen and Zen Classics*, vol. 2 (Tokyo: Hokuseidō, 1962) pp. 9–14. For more information on the Niu-t'ou school, see John R. MacRae, "The Ox-head School of Chinese Ch'an Buddhism," *Studies in Ch'an and Hua-yen* (Honolulu: University of Hawaii Press, 1983), pp. 169–252.

17. The dramatic rivalry between the two principal figures of Heian Buddhism is even the subject of an entire book entitled "Saichō or Kūkai? [Who is Tops?]": Terabayashi Shun, *Saichō ka Kūkai ka* (Tokyo: Keizaisha, 1986). For a comparison of the two Patriarchs in English see Allan G. Grapard, "Patriarchs of Heian Buddhism," *Great Historical Figures of Japan* (Tokyo: Japan Culture Institute, 1978) pp. 39–48 (his bias is toward Kūkai). The respective writings of Saichō and Kūkai are compared in Watanabe Shōkō ed., *Saichō-Kūkai* (Tokyo: Chikuma Shobō, 1986). For a full-length study of Kūkai see Yoshito S. Hakeda, *Kūkai: Major Works* (New York: Columbia University Press, 1972).

18. For particulars of the debate see Tamura Kōyū, "The Doctrinal Dispute between the Tendai and Hossō Sects" *Acta Asiatica*, no. 47, pp. 48–81, and Groner, pp. 91–106.

19. These precepts are described in the *Bonmyō-kyō*, no. 1484, in vol. 24, pp. 997–1011, in the standard reference the *Taishō daizō-kyō* (Tokyo: Daizō Shuppan Kabushiki Kaisha, 1924–1932).

20. For a translation of this little work see Groner, pp. 116–123.

21. Watanabe, *Saichō no kokoro to shōgai*, pp. 177–178.

22. For a discussion of Saichō's incorporation of Shintō into his Tendai system, see Alicia Matsunaga's *The Buddhist Philosophy of Assimilation* (Tokyo: Sophia/Tuttle, 1969), pp. 181–205.

THE MAGIC MOUNTAIN

1. There is very little in English on the history of Hiei. The Sanmon-Jimon split is discussed in Neil McMullin, "The Sanmon-Jimon Schism in the Tendai School of Buddhism: A Preliminary Analysis," *Journal of the International Association of Buddhist Studies*, vol. 7, no. 1 (Madison, 1984), pp. 83–106. In Japanese see Hazama Jikō, *Tendai-shū shi-gaisetsu* (Tokyo: Daizō Shuppan, 1977); Shibutani Jigai, *Tendai zasu ki* (Tokyo: Daiichi Shobō, 1939); and Kageyama Haruki et al., *Hiei-zan I*, Asahi Culture Books 60 (Osaka: Osaka Shoseki, 1986). For biographies of the main Tendai Patriarchs (Saichō, Ennin, Enchin, Ryōgen, and the contemporary marathon monk Sakai Yūsai) see Sonoda Kōyū, *Tendai-shū*.

2. Ennin is the subject of two books by Edwin O. Reischauer: *Ennin's Diary—The Record of a Pilgrimage to China in Search of the Law* and *Ennin's Travels in T'ang China*, both published in 1955 by the Roland Press of New York. Ennin's travels were also taken up by Arthur Waley,

"Ennin and Ensai," *The Real Tripitaka* (London: Allen & Unwin, 1952), pp. 131–168. An interesting study of Saichō and Ennin, with a chapter on the mountain marathon thrown in, is Yamanoue Sumio, *Hiei-zan kaisō* (Tokyo: Toki Shobō, 1986).

3. For information on Tendai esotericism see the profusely illustrated volume *Tendai mikkyō: shisō to bunka* (Sakamoto: Tendai-shūmūchō, 1973) and Michael Saso, "Kuden: The Oral Hermeneutics of Tendai Tantric Buddhism," *Japanese Journal of Religious Studies,* vol. 14, pp. 223–246. Also interesting is Stanley Weinstein's "The Beginning of Esoteric Buddhism in Japan: The Neglected Tendai Tradition," *Journal of Asian Studies,* vol. 34, no. 1 (1974), pp. 177–191.

4. *Denjutsu isshin kaimon, Dengyō daishi zenshū,* vol. 4 or 5 depending on the edition.

5. For the story of Japan's warrior-monks see: Katsuno Ryūshin, *Sōhei, Nihon rekishi shinsho* (Tokyo: Nihon Hankō-kai, 1965); Hioki Shōichi, *Nihon sōhei kenkyū* (Tokyo: Sanshō-dō, 1972); and Watanabe Shojun (Morimichi), *Sōhei seisui-ki* (Tokyo: Shibun-dō, 1984).

6. Quoted in Gouverneur Mosher, *Kyoto, A Contemplative Guide* (Tokyo: Tuttle, 1964), p. 37.

7. The three thousand temples of Hiei were said to have been distributed as follows: 1,813 in the Eastern Precinct, 717 in the Western Precinct, and 470 in the Yokawa Precinct. Recent excavation on the mountain brought about by the surge in reconstruction suggests that the devastation was not quite so extensive as previously thought. There is a legend that Hideyoshi, the Toyotomi general who assisted Nobunaga with the attack, let a number of priests secretly escape and that he even rescued some of the monastery treasures himself.

STUDY AND PRACTICE

1. In addition to Petzold's *Tendai Buddhism,* the *Japanese Journal of Religious Studies,* published by the Nanzan Institute for Religion and Culture in Nagoya, has put out a special "Tendai Buddhism in Japan" issue (vol. 14, nos. 2–3, June & September 1987). Recommended illustrated works in Japanese on Tendai Buddhism are *Hiei-zan Enryaku-ji* (Sakamoto: Enryaku-ji, 1963), Kageyama Haruki, *Hiei-zanji* (Kyoto: Dōbōsha, 1978); Nishigawa Isamu and Tanaka Hisao, *Saichō to Hiei-zan* (Tokyo: Kōsei Shuppansha, 1982); and "Hiei-zan to Tendai bijitsu," *Asahi Graphic Weekly* (March 25, 1986). Also good are Kageyama Haruki and Murayama Shuichi (eds.), *Hiei-zan: sono shūkyō to rekishi* (Tokyo: NHK books, 1970); Murayama Shuichi (ed.), *Hiei-zan to Tendai bukkyō no kenkyū* (Tokyo: Meichaku Shuppansha, 1975); Setouchi Jakushō et al., *Hiei-zan II* Osaka Culture Books 69 (Osaka: Osaka Shoseki, 1986); Gotō Chika et al., *Hiei-zan Enryaku-ji Sen-nihyaku-nen* (Tokyo: Shinchosha, 1986); and Watanabe Shujun et al., *Hiei-zan* (Tokyo: Hōzōkan, 1987). Nakayama Shobō (Yuishima 2-14-4, Bunkyo-ku, Tokyo) issues the interesting quarterly journal *Tendai.*

2. This quotation is the gist of one of Saichō's famous poems: *onozukara sumeba jikai no kono yama wa makoto naru ishin yori isho.*

3. *Sange-gakushō-shiki.*

4. *Konkairon, Dengyō daishi zenshū,* vol. 1.

5. *Sange-gakushō-shiki.*

6. For the relationship between Buddhism and social welfare see John Stevens, "Great Compassion: Mahāyāna Buddhism and Social Welfare," *Tohoku Fukushi University Twenty-fifth Anniversary Research Reports* (Sendai: Tohoku Fukushi University, 1984), pp. 181–191.

7. For a detailed discussion of the four kinds of *samādhi* see Daniel B. Stevenson, "The Four Kinds of Samadhi in Early T'ien-t'ai Buddhism," *Traditions of Meditation in Chinese Buddhism* (Honolulu: University of Hawaii Press, 1986), pp. 45–98.
8. Chap. 14, "A Happy Life."
9. See Tsukamoto Zenryū, "Buddhism and Fine Arts in Kyoto (II)," *Eastern Buddhist,* vol. 20, no. 1 (Spring 1987), pp. 62–75.
10. For a record of his experiences see Nakano Eiken, *Rōzan Juni-nen* (Kyoto: Nihon Bungeisha, 1970), and *Ichigu o ikiru* (Kyoto: Shirakawa Sho-in, 1976). In Take Kakuchō, "Hiei-zan no gyō", Watanabe et al., *Hiei-zan,* pp. 173–179, there is a list of all the twelve-year retreatants of the modern era.

MOUNT HIEI TODAY

1. Mosher's book, *Kyoto, A Contemplative Guide,* contains an excellent guide, with maps, of Hiei. A similar "contemplative" guide in Japanese is Kajiwara Gaku and Kikuchi Tōta, *Hiei-Zan* (Tokyo: Kōsei Shuppansha, 1986). Enryaku-ji puts out two excellent guides in Japanese—both entitled *Hiei-zan*—which are available at the souvenir stands on the mountain. An interesting modern short story on Hiei is Ri'ichi Yokomitsu's "Mount Hiei," translated by Lane Dunlop in *Translation,* vol. 17 (Fall, 1986), pp. 117–129.
2. A tremendous exhibition on Tendai art toured Japan to great acclaim during 1986. The catalogue, containing over 350 illustrations with summaries in English, is essential reading: *Hiei-zan to Tendai no bijutsu* (Tokyo: Asahi Shimbun-sha, 1986).
3. A nicely illustrated guidebook to Sakamoto is Kawasaki Tōru's *Monzen-machi Sakamoto* (Otsu: Ōmi Bunka-sha, 1980).

MOUNTAIN PILGRIMAGE

1. Major scholarly studies of *kaihōgyō* in Japanese include Hiramatsu Chōkū, *Hiei-zan kaihōgyō no kenkyū* (Tokyo: Miosha, 1982); Ōdera Bunei, "Hiei-zan kaihōgyō no shiteki tenkai," and Misaki Ryōshū, "Hiei-zan no kaihōgyō to sono rironteki konkyō," both in *Bukkyō ni okeru shūgyō to sono rironteki konkyō* (Tokyo: Nihon Bukkyō Gakkai, 1980); Murayama Shuichi, "Kaihōshugen-shi," *Hiei-zan I,* pp. 93–120; Mitsunaga Chōdō, "Sennichi kaihōgyō," *Hiei-zan II,* pp. 133–158; and Take Kakushō, "Sennichi kaihōgyō," *Hiei-zan,* pp. 157–169. In English there is an incredibly dull article on *kaihōgyō* in the *Japanese Journal of Religious Studies,* Tendai issue, vol. 14, nos. 2 & 3 (June & September 1987), pp. 185–202.
2. This occurs in the *Kongōchō-kyō (Taishō Daizō-kyō* (Skt. *Vajrasékhara-sūtra*), vol. 19, no. 957.) There is also a verse in the first chapter of the *Lotus Sūtra* extolling those "who, unsleeping, walk about the forest diligently seeking the Buddha Way" (translation by Katō et al.).

THE PATH OF THE SPIRITUAL ATHLETE

1. Nowadays the knife is usually carried only by the 1,000-day marathon monks.
2. The offering of *shikimi* branches at all the stations of worship along the route is called *kuge.*
3. In proper Sanskrit transliteration this runs: *namaḥ samanta vajrānaṁ caṇḍa mahāroṣaṇa sphoṭaya hūṁ traṭ hāṁmāṁ.* The meaning is something like "Hail to the Diamond Fire Kings,

the fearful Lords who terrorize evildoers; shatter too the darkness which lurks in my heart, O Holy Unshakable King of Light!"

4. The course is as follows: Hiei—Sekisan-in—Shinnyō-dō—Heian Shrine—Gyōja Bridge—Kiyomizu-dera—Gojō Tennin—Shinsen-in—Kitano Temman Shrine—Shimogamo Shrine—Kawai Shrine—Shōjōren-in.

5. An up-to-date list of the *gyōja* appears in Watanabe et al., *Hiei-zan,* pp. 163–166.

6. An account of the *lung-gom-pa* runners appears in Alexandra David-Neel's *Magic and Mystery in Tibet* (New York: Dover Publications, 1971), pp. 199–216.

7. For an excellent illustrated study of this important deity see *Fudō Myō-ō* (Kyoto: Hōzōkan, 1984).

RUNNING BUDDHAS

1. Much of the information on the early *gyōja* comes from Hagami Shōchō, *Dōshin,* revised edition, (Tokyo: Shunjūsha, 1971), pp. 239–266.

2. Genjun wrote of his experiences in "Hiei-zan kaihōgyō ni tsuite," *Gyō no bukkyō, Nihon seishin gyōsetsu,* vol. 5 (Tokyo: Sanshō-dō, 1939), pp. 1–25.

3. For a short biography of Hakozaki, see Kobayashi Ryūshō, "Fudō Myō-ō no gotoku ni ikiru; shinja de ari, gyōja de ari," *Tendai 4* (1981), pp. 25–31.

4. Among Hagami's many publications the following two books deal primarily with *kaihōgyō*: *Dōshin* (Tokyo: Shunjūsha, 1971), and *Ganshin* (Tokyo: Hōzōin, 1986). The second volume contains English translations of some of Hagami's talks delivered overseas.

5. Mitsunaga has written a book about his experiences: *Tada no hito to nare* (Tokyo: Yamanote Shobō, 1973). He is also featured together with Utsumi Shunshō in the illustrated book by Shirasu Misako and Gōtō Chikako, *Kaihōgyō* (Tokyo: Shinshin-dō, 1976) and has an article on *kaihōgyō* in Gotō et al., *Hiei-zan Enryakuji Sen-nihyaku-nen* (Tokyo: Shinchosha, 1986) pp. 80–91.

6. Utsumi is the centerpiece of the picture book *Hokurei no hito* by Hayashi Takashi and Murakami Mamoru (Tokyo: Kōsei Shuppansha, 1983). He was also the subject of a fascinating documentary film, *Yomigaeru Tōtō* ("Phoenix Mount Hiei") that was submitted to the U.S. Motion Picture Academy Awards in 1980. Unfortunately, it did not win.

7. Not surprisingly, Sakai is the subject of an ever-increasing number of books: Wazaki Nobuya, *Ajari Tanjō* (Tokyo: Kodansha, 1979); Nishigawa Isamu, *Gyō* (Tokyo: Kōdansha, 1981); Shima Kazuharu, *Gyōdō ni ikiru* (Tokyo: Kōsei Shuppansha, 1983); Kikuchi Tōta and Noki Shosuke, *Nisennichi kaihōgyō* (Tokyo: Kōsei Shuppansha, 1987); Shima Kazuharu, *Sakai Yūsai* (Tokyo: Shinjūsha, 1987); and a photo essay issued by the Imuro-kai, *Hokurei kaihōgyō: nisennichi mangyō kinen shashin-shū* (Osaka: Imuro-kai, 1987). NHK television, the Japanese national network, has produced several programs on Sakai.

8. Hiramatsu Chōkū, *Hiei-zan kaihōgyō-ki* (Tokyo: Miosha, 1981). The book contains many interesting photographs, which, unfortunately, are very poorly reproduced.

Bibliography

WORKS IN ENGLISH

Blyth, R. H. *Zen and Zen Classics,* vol. 2. Tokyo: Hokuseidō Press, 1964.

Chappell, David W. *T'ien-T'ai Buddhism: An Outline of the Fourfold Teachings.* Tokyo: Daiichi Shobō, 1983.

Ch'en, Kenneth. *Buddhism in China.* Princeton, N.J.: Princeton University Press, 1972.

————. *The Chinese Transformation of Buddhism.* Princeton, N.J.: Princeton University Press, 1973. This and the above volume by Ch'en give much information on the development of T'ien-t'ai in China.

Cleary, Thomas, trans. *The Flower Ornament Scripture.* 3 vols. Boston and London: Shambhala Publications, 1984–1987.

David-Neel, Alexandra. *Magic and Mystery in Tibet.* New York: Dover Publications, 1971.

De Visser, Marius W. *Ancient Buddhism in Japan.* Leiden: E. J. Brill, 1935.

Edkins, Joseph. *Chinese Buddhism.* London: Kegan Paul, Trench, Trubner & Co, 1893. (Reprinted New York, 1968). Contains a long section on T'ien-t'ai but marred by the Christian-missionary author's anti-Buddhist sentiments.

Eliot, Sir Charles. *Japanese Buddhism.* London: Edward Arnold, 1939.

Gimello, Robert M., and Peter N. Gregory, eds. *Studies in Ch'an and Hua-Yen.* Honolulu: University of Hawaii Press, 1983.

Grapard, Allan G. "Patriarchs of Heian Buddhism," in *Great Historical Figures of Japan,* pp. 39–48. Tokyo: Japan Culture Institute, 1978.

Gregory, Peter N., ed. *Traditions of Meditation in Chinese Buddhism.* Honolulu: University of Hawaii Press, 1986.

Groner, Paul. *Saichō.* Berkeley: Berkeley Buddhist Studies Series 7, 1984.

Hakeda, Yoshito S. *Kūkai: Major Works.* New York: Columbia University Press, 1972.

————, trans. *The Awakening of Faith.* New York: Columbia University Press, 1967.

Hurvitz, Leon. *Chih-i (538–597).* Brussels: Melanges et Bouddhiques, vol. 12, 1960–1962.

————, trans. *Scripture of the Lotus Blossom of the Fine Dharma.* New York: Columbia University Press, 1976.

BIBLIOGRAPHY

Katō, Bunnō et al., trans. *The Threefold Lotus Sutra.* New York and Tokyo: Weatherhill/Kosei, 1975.

Luk, Charles (Lu K'uan Yu). *The Secrets of Chinese Meditation.* York Beach, Me.: Weiser, 1984.

McMullin, Neil. "The Sammon-Jimon Schism in the Tendai School of Buddhism: A Preliminary Analysis." *Journal of the International Association of Buddhist Studies,* vol. 7, no. 1 (1984), pp. 83–106.

Matsunaga, Alicia. *The Buddhist Philosophy of Assimilation.* Rutland & Tokyo: Sophia/Tuttle, 1969.

Matsunaga, Daigan, and Alicia Matsunaga. *Foundations of Japanese Buddhism,* vols. 1 & 2. Los Angeles and Tokyo: Buddhist Books International, 1974–1976.

Mosher, Gouverneur. *Kyoto, A Contemplative Guide.* Rutland and Tokyo: Tuttle, 1964.

Murano, Senchū, trans. *The Lotus Sutra.* Tokyo: Nichiren-shu Headquarters, 1974.

Petzold, Bruno. *Tendai Buddhism.* Tokyo: International Buddhist Exchange Center, 1979.

Rambach, Pierre. *The Art of Japanese Tantricism.* London: Macmillan, 1979. While mostly on Shingon, the book does contain some material on Saichō and Tendai.

Reischauer, Edwin O. *Ennin's Diary—The Record of a Pilgrimage to China in Search of the Law.* New York: Ronald Press, 1955.

———. *Ennin's Travels in T'ang China.* New York: Ronald Press, 1955.

Rhodes, Robert, trans. "Saichō's Mappō Tōmyōki: The Candle of the Later Dharma." *Eastern Buddhist,* vol. 13, no. 1 (Spring, 1980), pp. 79–103.

Sangharakshita. *The Eternal Legacy.* London: Tharpa Publications, 1985. The study contains excellent explanations of the Mahāyāna texts used by Saichō.

Saunders, Dale E. *Buddhism in Japan.* Rutland and Tokyo: Tuttle, 1972.

Steinilber-Oberlin. *The Buddhist Sects of Japan.* London: Allen & Unwin, 1938.

Stevens, John. "Great Compassion: Mahāyāna Buddhism and Social Welfare," *Tohoku Fukushi University Twenty-fifth Anniversary Research Reports.* Sendai: Tohoku Fukushi University, 1984.

———. *Sacred Calligraphy of the East.* Boulder and London: Shambhala Publications, 1981. Contains a discussion of the importance of sutra-copying in the Buddhist tradition.

Swanson, Paul L., ed. "Tendai Buddhism in Japan." *Japanese Journal of Religious Studies,* vol. 14, nos. 2–3 (June–September 1987). This issue includes the following papers: "Why the *Lotus Sutra?*" (Whalen Lai); "The Characteristics of Japanese Tendai" (Hazama Jikō); "Inherent Enlightenment and Saichō's Acceptance of the Bodhisattva Precepts" (Shirato Waka); "Annen, Tankei, Henjō, and Monastic Discipline in the Tendai School" (Paul Groner); "The Enryaku-ji and Gion Shrine-Temple Complex in the Mid-Heian Period" (Neil McMullin); "The *Kaihōgyō* Practice of Mt. Hiei" (Robert F. Rhodes); "Japanese Culture and the Tendai Concept of Original Enlightenment" (Tamura Yoshiro); "Linguistic Cubism—A Singularity of Pluralism in the Sannō Cult" (Allan Grapard); "*Kūden:* The Oral Hermeneutics of Tendai Tantric Buddhism" (Michael Saso); and "Is Tendai Buddhism Relevant to the Modern World?" (David W. Chappell).

BIBLIOGRAPHY

Takakusa, Junjirō. *The Essentials of Buddhist Philosophy.* Honolulu: University of Hawaii Press, 1956.

Takasaki, Jikido, ed. *Acta Asiatica,* no. 47. Tokyo: Tōhō Gakkai, 1985.

Tsukamoto Zenryū. "Buddhism and Fine Arts in Kyoto (II)." *Eastern Buddhist,* vol. 20, no. 1 (Spring 1987), pp. 62–80.

Ui Hakuju. "A Study of Japanese Tendai Buddhism." *Philosophical Studies of Japan,* no. 1 (Tokyo, 1959).

van Gulik, R. H. *Siddham.* New Delhi: Mrs. Sharada Rani, 1980. Contains a section on Sanskrit studies within Japanese Tendai.

Waley, Arthur. *The Real Tripitaka and Other Pieces.* London: Allen & Unwin, 1952.

Watanabe, Shōkō. *Japanese Buddhism.* Tokyo: Japanese Cultural Society, 1970.

Watson, Burton, trans. *Cold Mountain.* New York: Columbia University Press, 1970.

Weinstein, Stanley. "The Beginnings of Esoteric Buddhism in Japan. The Neglected Tendai Tradition." *Journal of Asian Studies,* vol. 34, no. 1 (1974), pp. 177–191.

Yamamoto Kōshō. *The Mahāyāna Mahāparinirvāṇa Sūtra.* 3 vols. Ube: Karinbunko, 1973–1975.

Yokomitsu, Ri'ichi, and Lane Dunlop, trans. "Mount Hiei." *Translation.* vol. 22, (Fall 1986), pp. 117–29.

WORKS IN JAPANESE

Asahi Shimbun, ed. "Hiei-zan to Tendai bijutsu." *Asahi Graphic Weekly,* March 25, 1986.

———. *Hiei-zan to Tendai no bijutsu* (Exhibition Catalogue). Tokyo: Asahi Shimbunsha, 1986.

Bukkyō Gakkai, ed. *Bukkyō in okeru shugyō to sono rironteki konkyo.* Tokyo: Bukkyō Gakkai, 1980.

Enryaku-ji, ed. *Hiei-zan Enryaku-ji.* Sakamoto: Enryaku-ji, 1963.

Fukuda Gōyei. *Tendai-gaku gairon.* 2 vols. Tokyo: Bunichi Shuppansha, 1954–59.

Gotō, Chikao et al. *Hiei-zan Enryakuji Sen-nihyaku-nen* Tokyo: Shinchosha, 1986. An inexpensive, excellent introduction to Tendai Buddhism illustrated with color photographs.

Hagami Shōchō. *Dōshin.* Tokyo: Shunjūsha, 1971.

———. *Ganshin.* Tokyo: Hōzōin, 1986.

Hayashi Takashi and Murakami Mamoru. *Hokurei no hito.* Tokyo: Kōsei Shuppansha, 1983.

Hazama Jikō. *Tendai-shū shigaisetsu.* Tokyo: Daizō Shuppan, 1977.

Hiei-san Senshu-in, ed. *Dengyō daishi zenshū.* Various editions.

Hioki Shōichi. *Nihon sōhei kenkyū.* Tokyo: Sanshō-dō, 1972.

Hirakawa Akira. *Saichō.* Tokyo: Shūeisha, 1985.

Hiramatsu Chōkū. *Hiei-zan kaihōgyō no kenkyū.* Tokyo: Miosha, 1982.

———. *Hiei-zan kaihōgyō-ki.* Tokyo: Miosha, 1981.

Imuro-kai. *Hokurei kaihōgyō nisennichi mangyō kinen shashin-shū.* Osaka: Imuro-kai, 1987.

Kageyama Haruki. *Hiei-zan ji.* Kyoto: Dōbōsha, 1978.

——— et al. *Hiei-zan I.* Asahi Culture Books 60. Osaka: Osaka Shoseki, 1986.

——— and Murayama Shuichi, ed. *Hiei-zan: sono shūkyō to rekishi.* Tokyo: NHK Books, 1970.

Kajiwara Gaku and Kikuchi Tōta. *Hiei-zan.* Tokyo: Kōsei Shuppansha, 1986.

Katsuno Ryūshin. *Sōhei.* Tokyo: Nihon Hankokai, 1965.

Kawasaki Tōru. *Monzen-mae machi Sakamoto.* Otsu: Ōmi Bunkasha, 1980.

Kikuchi Tōta and Noki Shosuke. *Nisennichi kaihōgyō.* Tokyo: Kōsei Shuppansha, 1987.

Kiuchi Hiroshi. *Dengyō daishi no shōgai to shisō.* Tokyo: Daisan-bunmeisha, 1976.

Mibun Taishun and Miyasaka Yūshō. *Tendai-Shingon.* Tokyo: Shinjūsha, 1971.

Mitsunaga Chōdō. *Tada no hito to nare.* Tokyo: Yamanote Shobō, 1973.

Murayama Shūichi, ed. *Hiei-zan to Tendai bukkyō no kenkyū.* Tokyo: Meicho Shuppansha, 1975.

Nagai Michiko. *Saichō o tadaru.* Tokyo: Kōdansha, 1987. She has also written a historical novel based on the life of Saichō: *Kumo to kaze* (Tokyo: Chuō Koronsha, 1987).

Nakano Eiken. *Ichigu o ikiru.* Kyoto: Shirakawa Shoin, 1976.

———. *Rōzan juninen.* Kyoto: Nihon Bungeisha, 1970.

Nakayama Shobō. *Tendai.* Quarterly journal, 1980–.

Nishikawa Isamu. *Gyō.* Tokyo: Kōdansha, 1981.

——— and Tanaka Hisao. *Saichō to Hiei-zan.* Tokyo: Kōsei Shuppansha, 1982.

Okuno Genjun. "Hiei-zan kaihōgyō ni tsuite, *Gyō no Bukkyō,* Nihon seishin gyōsetsu, vol. 5, pp. 1–25. Tokyo: Sanshō-dō, 1935.

Sekiguchi Shindai. *Tendai kyōgaku no kenkyū.* Tokyo: Daitō Shuppansha, 1978.

———. *Tendai shō-shikan.* Tokyo: Daitō Shuppansha, 1978.

Setouchi Jakushō et al. *Hiei-zan II.* Osaka Culture Books 69. Osaka: Osaka Shoseki, 1986.

Shibutani Jigai. *Tendai zasu-ki.* Tokyo: Daiichi Shobō, 1939.

Shima Kazuharu. *Gyōdō ni ikiru.* Tokyo: Kōsei Shuppansha, 1983.

———. *Sakai Yūsai.* Tokyo: Shunjūsha, 1987.

Shiori Ryōdō and Kikuchi Gyō-ō, eds. *Saichō.* Tokyo: Yoshikawa Kobunkan, 1982.

Shirasu Misako and Gōtō Chikako. *Kaihōgyō.* Tokyo: Shinshinsha, 1976.

Sonoda Kōyū. *Tendai-shū.* Tokyo: Shogakkan, 1986.

——— and Andō Toshio. *Saichō.* Tokyo: Iwanami Shoten, 1974.

Tendai Gakkai, ed. *Dengyō daishi kenkyū.* Tokyo: Waseda Daigaku Shuppan-bu, 1973.

Tendai-shūmūchō, ed. *Tendai mikkyō: shisō to bunka.* Sakamoto: Tendai-shū, 1973.

Terabayashi Shun. *Saichō ka Kūkai ka.* Tokyo: Keizaisha, 1986.

Uesugi Bunshu. *Nihon Tendai-shi.* 2 vols. Tokyo: Kokusho Hankōkai, 1973.

Umehara Takeshi. *Saichō meisō.* Tokyo: Kōsei Shuppansha, 1987.

Watanabe, Shojun. *Saichō no kokoro to shōgai.* Tokyo: Yūzan 1977.

———. *Sōhei seisui-ki.* Tokyo: Shibun-dō, 1984.

——— et al. *Hiei-zan.* Tokyo: Hōzōin, 1987.

BIBLIOGRAPHY

Watanabe Shōkō, ed. *Saichō-Kūkai*. Tokyo: Chikuma Shobō, 1986.

Wazaki Nobuya. *Ajari no Tanjō*. Tokyo: Kōdansha, 1979.

Yamada Etai. *Dōshin wa kuni no takara*. Tokyo: Kōsei Shuppansha, 1987.

——. *Hokke-kyō to dengyō daishi*. Tokyo: Daiichi Shobō, 1973.

Yamanoue Sumio. *Hiei-zan kaisō*. Tokyo: Toki Shobō, 1986.

Yomiuri Shimbun. *Saichō to Tendai bukkyō*. Tokyo: Yomiuri Shimbunsa, 1987. A lavishly illustrated introduction to Saichō and Tendai Buddhism. Includes photographs of the twelve-year retreat at Jōdō-in, articles about Sakai and Utsumi, and descriptions, with illustrations, of the Four Practices of Tendai.

Glossary

Ajari (Skt. *ācārya*). Tendai priests who have completed one of the great practices of Hiei are honored with the title *Ajari,* meaning "saintly master." In the case of the marathon monks, they become *ajari* upon completion of *dōiri,* earning the right to wear a black hem on their white robes (which also facilitates distinguishing between a trainee monk and a master). The term *ajari* is somewhat akin to the Zen Buddhist *rōshi* but carries more weight since the title is more difficult to attain. Senior marathon monks are addressed as *Ajari-sama,* the *-sama* being a more polite form of the honorific suffix *-san.*

Aka-i (Skt. *argha, arghya*). *Aka* is the name of the sacred well (*i*) near Myō-ō-dō that is used for the *dōiri shusui* ritual.

Amida Butsu (Skt. *Amitābha Buddha*). Amida is the Buddha of Infinite Light and Life. This Buddha, Lord of the Western Paradise, vowed to save all those who invoke his name. He is the principal Buddha of the Pure Land schools.

Bodhicitta (Jap. *dōshin, bodaishin*). This quality, "a mind set on being awakened," is the basis of all Buddhist practice. While the expression of *bodhicitta* differs from system to system, the fundamental aspiration is the same for Buddhists of any era or place. Saichō considered *bodhicitta* the greatest of all human attributes.

Byakutai Gyōja. A marathon monk who has completed five 100-day terms. He is given a special white belt to wear and may use a staff thereafter to help him negotiate his way through the mountains.

Daigyōman Ajari. Upon completion of the full 1,000-day term, the marathon monk is proclaimed a Saintly Master of the Highest Practice. A *Daigyōman Ajari* is popularly looked up to as a "living Buddha" who teaches by example and possesses great spiritual insight.

Dainichi Nyorai (Skt. *Mahāvairocana Tathāgata*). The Great Primordial Sun Buddha who expounds the esoteric teaching; all the other Buddhas and Bodhisattvas emanate from Dainichi—the entire universe constitutes his form. Dainichi is the principal Buddha of the Tantric schools.

Deva. Hindu deity. Many such gods were incorporated into the Buddhist pantheon.

Dhammapada. A basic Buddhist text, containing a series of aphorisms setting out the path to enlightenment. Although originally used primarily by the Theravāda, the *Dhammapada* has become, through the vehicle of translation, a standard work for Buddhists of all persuasions.

[147]

Dōiri. The "entry into the hall" at Myō-ō-dō, a nine-day (182-hour) confinement with no water, food, rest, or sleep. It occurs immediately after the marathon monk completes day 700. Variations of *dōiri* are conducted on some of the other mountains associated with Shugendō.

Dōnin. In the old system, *dōnin*, "the men of the halls," were the lower-ranking priests on Hiei who conducted the regular religious rites.

Dōshin. See *Bodhicitta.*

Dōshū. "Mass regulars," another name for *dōnin.*

Dosoku sandai. Upon completion of the full 1,000-day term, the marathon monk is "invited to the palace with his straw sandals on" to conduct a service for the imperial household. The monk may walk the corridors of the Kyoto Imperial Palace without removing his footwear, the only person in Japan allowed to do so. When the emperor was reigning in Kyoto the ceremony was performed in front of the imperial household; nowadays, with the capital in Tokyo, the emperor and his family attend in absentia. The occasion is extremely formal, with hundreds of Buddhist and Shintō priests turned out in all their finery in a spectacular display of medieval pagentry.

Ekō-ryū. The formal name of the Imuro Valley marathon course.

Fudō Myō-ō (Skt. *Acala Vidyārāja*). Fudō, the fiery Unshakable One, is the esoteric deity that the marathon monks venerate and attempt to identify with. Surrounded by cosmic flames that consume evil and passions, Fudō smites the wicked while imparting wisdom to those who acknowledge his presence as a manifestation of Dainichi Nyorai. The cult of Fudō is very strong in Japanese Buddhism. Philosophically, Fudō represents the state of being fixed between all opposition, unshakably set right in the center of the ceaseless whirl of existence.

Fugen Bosatsu (Skt. *Samantabhadra Bodhisattva*). This Bodhisattva, who represents the meditation and practice of Buddhism, often appears in visions to the marathon monks.

Gakushō (or *Gakuto*). In the old system, these were the higher-ranking priests drawn from aristocratic or warrior families. The *gakushō* were supposed to engage in advanced study and training and serve as middle-echelon administrators.

Gegyō Jishu. "Intellectual Training" i.e., study of the sutras, ceremonies, and other Tendai rites. Always paired with *shidō kegyō jishu.*

Goma (Skt. *homa*). The vedic fire ceremony (*homa*) was incorporated into Tantric Buddhism; symbolizing the fire of wisdom that consumes all passions and purifies the world, the Buddhist *goma* is a central element of both Tendai and Shingon.

Goma no ken. "The dagger that drives away Mara" is carried by the marathon monks to remind them of their vow to commit suicide if they fail to complete any part of the training. The name of the dagger refers to the tale of the demon Mara attacking Śākyamuni as he sat beneath the Bo (or Bodhi) Tree. Incidentally, during the American occupation of Japan, possession of any type of weapon was strictly outlawed, and the marathon monks had to apply for a special exemption. Even today there are problems with the police about carrying a "concealed weapon"; consequently only the 1,000-day marathon monks take along the *goma no ken* on their rounds. The 100-day marathon monks must rely exclusively on the "cord of death" if it becomes necessary to honor their vow.

Gyōja (Skt. *ācārin*). One who undergoes strict Buddhist training. "Ascetic" is another possible translation of the term, but the meaning of *gyōja* is more positive—one is "moving" along the path of awakening, for both oneself and others, and not recoiling from the world in horror and abject abnegation.

Gyokusen-ryū. The formal name of the Mudō-ji Valley marathon course.

Hangyō-hanza sammai. "Half-sitting, half-standing *samādhi*" is one of the four classical practices of Tendai. Although it was practiced in different forms over the centuries, it typically consists of alternating the chanting of the *Lotus Sūtra* while circumambulating and meditating on the text's contents while sitting. The length of the practice was generally from twenty-one to twenty-eight days.

Higasa. The special trademark hat of the mountain monks. Its lotus leaf shape is a symbol of Fudō Myō-ō, the monks' patron, and is thus treated with the utmost respect—it may not even be worn on the head until the *gyōja* has put in 300 days of training.

Hisen. The stand used to hold the *higasa* when it is necessary to set it down.

Hiza-higyō sammai. "Not sitting, not moving *samādhi*," one of the four classic Tendai practices, is formless: a state in which all of one's daily actions are conducted with total presence of mind. Since this is extremely difficult to achieve, this "practice of no-practice" is only for the wisest and most advanced *gyōja*.

Hō-no-yū. A medicinal drink, concocted from the bark of the *hōnoki* (*magnolia obovata*), given to the *gyōja* at the end of *dōiri* to revive him.

Ichigassui. A secret rite performed at a waterfall near Sakamoto by the marathon monks once during a 100-day term. The rite, said to have originated with the founder of *kaihōgyō*, Sō-ō, is for driving out the disease and illness that exist in the village by having them flow away in the surrounding streams.

Inge. In the old system, the abbots of the Hiei subtemples. *Inge* were almost exclusively cloistered noblemen, many of whom remained embroiled in temporal affairs, an unfortunate situation that eventually led to Hiei's destruction in 1571.

Inka. A document issued by a Zen master, certifying that a pupil has completed his or her training.

Innen (Skt. *hetu-pratyana*). *Innen*, "karmic affinity," is a key concept of Japanese Buddhism. *In* is the inner impetus that causes one to study Buddhism; *en* are the relationships that subsequently arise. *Innen* is not fatalism since, in the Buddhist scheme of things, events are not predetermined—no one can predict the eventual results—and are never set, not even for an instant.

Jimon. This is the "Temple Branch" of Tendai, in contrast to the "Mountain Branch" of Hiei, headquartered at Onjō-ji. The split between the two branches occurred in the Middle Ages and has never been effectively healed, not even in today's atmosphere of ecumenical goodwill.

GLOSSARY

Jōgyō-sammai. "Continuous-walking *samādhi,*" one of the four Tendai practices, consists of 90 days of seclusion while ceaselessly chanting the *nembutsu.* In limbo for more than a hundred years, it has recently been reestablished on Hiei.

Jōza-sammai. "Continuous-sitting *samādhi,*" one of the four Tendai practices, involves 90 days of *shikan* meditation.

Jumanmai daigoma. In this eight-day Great Fire Ceremony, the *gyōja* sits constantly before a roaring cauldron, casting into the flames prayer-stick after prayer-stick. Various petitions are inscribed on the sticks, and the *gyōja* is relaying the message, so to speak, to Fudō Myō-ō. The *gyōja* must abstain from water and food, but unlike *dōiri* he is permitted periods of rest. This is the last trial of the marathon monks, generally undertaken two or three years following completion of a 1,000-day term.

Kaihōgyō. The "practice of circling the mountains"—translated in the book as "mountain marathon"—is an ancient Buddhist tradition likely dating back to the time of Śākyamuni. Hiei *kaihōgyō* is a pilgrimage to the sacred sites of the mountain and an appreciation of the principles represented in each respective station of worship. *Kaihōgyō* is also performed at most of the other holy mountains in Japan.

Katsuragawa Geango. This important summer retreat is held annually at Katsuragawa Valley, located about 40 kilometers north of Hiei. Every *gyōja* who has completed a 100-day term of *kaihōgyō* is eligible to attend the retreat. A *gyōja* who attends eight or more times earns the title of *Sendatsu,* "Master"; one who makes the retreat fiften or more times is a *Daisendatsu,* "Great Master"; and those rare souls who go more than twenty-five times become *Daidaisendatsu,* the "Greatest of Masters."

Kirimawari. Also known as the *Kyōto Kirimawari,* this is the special one-day run through Kyoto held each year. A senior *gyōja* leads a large procession, consisting of his disciples and lay followers, along the 54-kilometer Kyoto course. In addition to the regular stops, they visit a number of parishioners' homes along the way to perform short prayer services. Due to the extended program, the run often requires up to twenty hours.

Kōsōgyō. In order to "visualize the Buddha," a *gyōja* will seclude himself in a hall and spend twelve to thirteen hours a day chanting the names of each of the 3,000 Buddhas nonstop until he actually perceives them with his own eyes. There is no set length for the practice, but typically there is breakthrough between the eightieth and nintieth day. The *gyōja,* who must insist on undergoing the practice under his own volition, is carefully watched at all times, and his "vision" must be validated by a council of senior priests.

Kuge. The offering of *shikimi* branches to each of the main stations of worship.

Kunin. In the old system, these were the married lay brothers who served as sacristans, gatekeepers, carpenters, and gardeners; the ranks of the *kunin* were eventually infiltrated by brigands and ne'er-do-wells, the group that became the core of Hiei's dreaded *sōhei,* or warrior-monks.

Lung-gom-pa (rlung-sgom-pa). Tibetan marathon monks of extraordinary swiftness.

Maegyō. A period of preparatory training. In the case of *kaihōgyō,* it is the week preceding the first day of the marathon. The *gyōja* puts his affairs in order, prepares the necessary accessories, and develops a proper frame of mind. For the Jumanmai Daigoma, maegyō begins 100 days before the ceremony; most kinds of food are prohibited, and the *gyōja* lives on nuts, buckwheat paste, potatoes, and pine needles.

Mangyō. "Fulfillment of the practice," i.e., the last day of the full term.

Mikkyō. The Tantric teaching of Buddhism, involving the full spectrum of techniques to foster realization. *Mikkyō* is secret in the sense of not being suitable for everybody, and therefore not taught openly. In Tendai, priests usually select the *shikan* meditation course or the esoteric *mikkyō* course.

Namu Amida Butsu. "Hail to Amitābha Buddha," the *nembutsu* chant.

Nembutsu. This is the act of invoking Amitābha Buddha's name. Amitābha, the Buddha of Infinite Light and Life, is Lord of the Western Paradise, determined to save anyone who thinks of Him wholeheartedly. On the highest levels, through the practice of the *nembutsu* one recognizes the Western Paradise within one's own mind, the Pure Land where Buddha and the practitioner are one. All of the Japanese Pure Land schools evolved from Tendai.

Nobakama. The white trousers worn by the marathon monks.

Ōmawari. The aptly named Great Marathon, which occurs between the 800th and 900th days of *sennichi kaihōgyō.* The entire run is 84 kilometers, covering the holy sites on both Hiei and Kyoto.

Rōzan. Mountain retreat. In Tendai today there is the three-year mountain retreat, for those who hope to become an abbot of a Hiei subtemple, and a twelve-year retreat for *sennichi kaihōgyōja* and the hermits who serve at Jōdō-in. Saichō recommended *rōzan* for all Tendai students; one could pursue his training high in the clouds, far above the turmoil of the world below.

Saijiki-gi. The "farewell meal" given by the other abbots of Hiei for a marathon monk who is undertaking *dōiri.*

Saitō. The Western Precinct of Hiei, containing five of the mountain's sixteen valleys: Higashi, Nishi, Nishio, Kitao, and Kita.

Sammon. The "Mountain Branch" of Tendai, centered on Hiei. The Jimon Branch is headquartered at Onjō-ji.

Sekisan kugyō. The 60-kilometer Sekisan Marathon is performed in the sixth year of *sennichi kaihōgyō,* from days 700 to 800. The regular Hiei course is lengthened to include a stop at Sekisan Zen-in, a temple at the base of Hiei on the Kyoto side. Since that stop doubles the length of the daily run, it is called *kugyō,* "severe practice." The Sekisan Marathon is good preparation for the following year's Ōmawari.

Sekisen-ryū. The formal name of the Shōgyōbō course in the Western Precinct; it has been abandoned since the seventeenth century.

Sennichi kaihōgyō. The 1,000-day mountain marathon of Mount Hiei, broken up into ten 100-day terms over a seven-year period.

Shakamuni Nyorai (Skt. *Śākyamuni Tathāgata*). The historical Buddha. He is the principal Buddha of the Lotus schools.

Shakyō. Sutra-copying, one of the oldest of Buddhist devotional practices, praised by the *Lotus Sutra. Shakyō* is an important element of classical Tendai training.

Shide-no-himo. The "cord of death" carried around the waist of all marathon monks, to be used by the runner to hang himself if he fails to complete any part of the training.

Shidō kegyō jishu. "Applied training," the second pillar of Tendai studies, involving implementation of theoretical learning.

Shikan (Skt. *śamatha-vipaśyanā*). Tendai-style meditation of "calming the mind and discerning the Real."

Shikimi. Japanese star anise (*Illicium religiosum*), a plant widely grown in Buddhist temples for use as an altar and tombstone offering. Marathon monks carry the branches to offer to the stations of worship along the route.

Shingyōja. A rookie marathon monk in his first 100-day term.

Shishū sammai. The four *samādhi*s of Tendai Buddhism: (1) *jōgyō sammai* (2) *jōza sammai* (3) *hangyō hanza sammai* and (4) *higyō hiza sammai*.

Shojin ryōri. "Food for practice," vegetarian Buddhist fare.

Shugendō. This is a complex religious phenomenon, an amalgamation of mountain worship, Shintō, esoteric Buddhism, and Taosim. Hiei *sennichi kaihōgyō* is a type of Shugendō that also embraces elements of "moving Zen" and strict adherence to the monastic precepts.

Shusui. The water-taking ritual performed during *dōiri*, in which the *gyōja* draws water from the Aka Well and carries it back to the temple to offer to Fudō Myō-ō.

Sokuhō-kō. The "sodality" or community that supports the marathon monks. The official *sokuhō-kō*, distinguished by traditional costumes and paper lanterns, is an ancient institution, and the positions in it are largely hereditary.

Tabi. Japanese-style socks with a separation between the first and second toes.

Taikomawashi (or *taiko-nori*). A festive ceremony held during the Katsuragawa Summer Retreat. New *gyōja* leap onto a huge revolving drum and then fly into a crowd of lay believers in emulation of their Patriarch Sō-ō's dramatic jump into the Katsuragawa Falls to embrace his vision of Fudō Myō-ō.

Taimitsu. The Tendai system of Tantric Buddhism.

Takigyō. "Waterfall practice," i.e., standing under a waterfall and chanting prayers in order to purify oneself. It is an ancient religious practice in Japan, mentioned in the earliest of chronicles.

Tathāgata. Alternate title for a Buddha, meaning one who is "thus come" on the path of realization.

Tebumi. The handwritten manual each marathon monk carries, giving him all the pertinent information concerning the route.

Tokudō. "Attaining the Way," i.e., Buddhist ordination.

Tōmitsu. The Shingon system of Tantric Buddhism.

Tōtō. The Eastern Precinct of Hiei, the first to be developed, containing five of the mountain's sixteen valleys: Minami, Kita, Higashi, Nishi, and Mudō-ji.

GLOSSARY

Yakushi Nyorai (Skt. *Bhaiṣajya Tathāgata*). The Buddha of healing. Yakushi was Saichō's patron deity, dedicated to curing the physical and spiritual ailments of all sentient beings.

Yamabushi. "Mountain priests," often self-ordained, who practice esoteric rites on sacred peaks. The creed of the *yamabushi* is an amalgamation of Shintoism, Taoism, esoteric Buddhism, and folk religion.

Yokawa. The third Precinct of Hiei, the last to be developed and traditionally the most remote and impoverished. It contains six of the mountain's sixteen valleys: Tosotsu, Kabo, Hannya, Imuro, Kaishin, and Gedatsu.

Zasu. Supreme abbot of Enryaku-ji and Primate of the Tendai sect.

Index

Page numbers in italic type refer to illustrations

INDEX

About the author

John Stevens is Professor of Buddhist Studies
and Aikido Instructor at Tohoku College of
Social Welfare in Sendai, Japan.